M000042429

CHILDREN *Are* A BLESSING *from the* LORD

CHILDREN *Are* A BLESSING *from the* LORD

Learning God's Wisdom Through Our Children

Tamara Boggs

kregel
PUBLICATIONS

Grand Rapids, MI 49501

Children Are a Blessing from the Lord: Learning God's Wisdom Through Our Children

© 2001 by Tamara Boggs

Published by Kregel Publications, a division of Kregel, Inc., P.O. Box 2607, Grand Rapids, MI 49501. For more information about Kregel Publications, visit our web site: www.kregel.com.

All rights reserved. No part of this book may be reproduced, stored in a retrieval system, or transmitted in any form or by any means—electronic, mechanical, photocopy, recording, or otherwise—without written permission of the publisher, except for brief quotations in printed reviews.

Unless otherwise noted, Scripture quotations are from the *Holy Bible, New International Version®.* © 1973, 1978, 1984 by International Bible Society. Used by permission of Zondervan Publishing House. All rights reserved.

Scripture quotations marked KJV are from the King James version of the Holy Bible.

Cover design: John M. Lucas

Library of Congress Cataloging-in-Publication Data
Boggs, Tamara.
    Children are a blessing from the Lord: learning God's wisdom through our children / Tamara Boggs.
        p.   cm.
    1. Parents—Prayer books and devotions—English.
2. Parenting—Religious aspects—Christianity—
Meditations. I. Title.
BV4845 .B64   2001   242'.645—dc21   2001029024
                                         CIP

ISBN 0-8254-2065-2

Printed in the United States of America

1 2 3 4 5 / 05 04 03 02 01

To
Nathaniel,
Christiana, and Hannah

CONTENTS

Foreword by Gloria Gaither 9
Acknowledgments 13
Introduction 15

Day 1:   Laps in Love 19
Day 2:   Organic Parenting 22
Day 3:   Learning to Climb 25
Day 4:   A Space of My Own 28
Day 5:   The Puzzle of My Life 32
Day 6:   Disconnected from the Stem 36
Day 7:   Love and Hammers 39
Day 8:   Jesus off the Cross 42
Day 9:   Jesus in Traction 46
Day 10:   "I Don't Want You to Miss Me" 50
Day 11:   "My Name is Nathaniel Boggs" 53
Day 12:   Steel Wool and Turpentine 57
Day 13:   Stay Close 60
Day 14:   The Wind Beneath My Kite 65
Day 15:   Keep Dancing 70
Day 16:   Knowing It All 74
Day 17:   Singing Along 77
Day 18:   Baby Teeth 80
Day 19:   "Can I Go Now?" 84
Day 20:   Moonwalkers 88
Day 21:   Meaning to Memories 92

Day 22: Too Many Questions 96
Day 23: Weed Harvesting 100
Day 24: Unbearable Punishment 103
Day 25: Paint Rollers and Messy Walls 107
Day 26: Dirty Feet 112
Day 27: Disabled Dreams 116
Day 28: Not Afraid to Shine 120
Day 29: It's Not Yours 124
Day 30: The Pizza of Life 129
Day 31: The Light of the World 132

Conclusion 137

OREWORD

At seven o'clock on Monday mornings, a rag-tag bunch of heart-hungry women gather at a log cabin in the woods. We bring whatever we have handy—an orange, a couple of apples, half a loaf of cranberry bread, a few boiled eggs—and we have coffee by the crackling fire. In winter it is still dark that early, but something important, something we all have in common, drags us from our homes to this quite hidden meeting place. We share a deep longing to know God.

For seven years now, these friends have borne each other's burdens in prayer and studied the living Word to discover the character and intent of Jesus. In this pursuit we have discovered a great deal about the character and intent of each other as well.

One of these Monday morning seekers is a tall, raven-haired young mother named Tamara Boggs. I had come to know Tamara because her husband, Don (head of the communications department at Anderson University), spent a great deal of time with my husband, Bill Gaither, in the video edit suite of Covenant Productions, editing together the first thirty or so of the *Homecoming Video Series.* The biggest thing Tamara and I had in common back then was that we were both "video widows."

And at first I thought she was shy. But as we began to pray, explore, and question the issues of life together, I discovered that she was both refreshingly deep and simple. She was willing to question everything yet take the wisdom of her own children over the cynicism of all-too-seasoned "theologians." It was her style to wait while we all had our say—each of us sort of spewing out at random whatever reactions came to our minds—then she would slowly begin to assimilate and distill all our "streams of consciousness" into formidable deductions that we could hold up for illumination in the light of God's Word.

Often Tamara would use a story as fresh as "this morning" about her children and the unique challenges they presented to her. Or some simple phrase surprised us all into one of those "duh!" moments when the answer was so obvious and simple that we'd walked right over it in pursuit of something harder and more complicated.

God and truth are like that. How human of us to think "profound" is synonymous with "difficult." It is almost never the case.

Jesus was the Master of pointing out profound truths with a simple illustration. While Pharisees argued obscure tenets of the Law, Jesus spoke worlds of revelation with a lump of clay, a tiny seed, words written in the dust, a towel and basin, a bushel basket and a candle.

When I was a new mother, I thought, "There goes my devotional life! So much for spiritual discoveries! I'll never have a quiet time for a profound thought again." In a way, I was right. But what I got instead was amazing gems of wisdom and blinding lasers of truth right on my "road to Damascus"—while folding laundry, bathing wiggly bodies, scrambling dozens of eggs, or tucking blankets around pajamaed little shoulders.

- "Mommy, did you know rainbows live at Easter?"
- "Grandmas are for sharing a piece of the moon."
- "Amy, there's more than air out there. There's love out there, and you can *feel* it."

- "I can't! I'm getting *little.*"
- "Is there a place where babies wait before they come to be?"

These, and a thousand other "devotionals," sent me to search for answers to questions I would never have asked had I not had three tiny emissaries "so lately come from God."

This is how I know that this book of moments from my friend Tamara is not for "mommies only." It is for anyone who longs for fresh insights from the heart of a seeker in sneakers.

—GLORIA GAITHER

CKNOWLEDGMENTS

My first and last thanks goes to my husband, Don, who believes in me and hopes for me when my eyes are dimmed by the complexities of our lives. God has blessed me beyond measure in sharing the parenting of our children and all of life with you.

Thank you, Brent, for teaching me much about the craft of writing and for persistently calling me "writer" until I believed you.

My deep appreciation to Gloria Gaither and the women of Monday-morning Bible study. You have prayed this book into being.

Thanks to Dennis, Steve, Janyre, Sarah, and all the good folks at Kregel who saw the ministry potential of this book. May these words indeed return to glorify God with a manyfold harvest in the hearts of those who share this journey.

INTRODUCTION

The organist played a Bach prelude as my husband, my three children, and I filed into the second-row pew at church. The kids scooted back and forth until settled into their worship service territories.

Having claimed her turn to sit next to Mom, Christiana scrunched close and whispered, "Is it family reunion today?"

I thought I misheard and motioned for her to try again. She pointed to the altar table laid with trays of the sacrament for the Communion service. Her tone intensified to a stage whisper. "Is it family reunion today?"

I smiled to myself as I realized what Christiana was saying. Communion a "family reunion"? Of course. But I hadn't thought of it that way until my daughter tangled her terms.

Not every spiritual insight received from my children has been as humorous. Some lessons learned through being a parent have come from facing my inadequacies and seeing myself as a wholly dependent child of God. But each lesson has been a precious gift from my heavenly parent toward growth.

Several years before receiving the Communion lesson from Christiana, I struggled with the constant collision of parenting demands and my need for spiritual nourishment. My pre-parenting methods of faith development and maintaining my relationship with God weren't working.

One night, I sat in the recliner in my living room listening to Christiana screaming and crying in her bedroom for me to come. I felt exhausted and frustrated. I feared Christiana's crying would wake her four-year-old brother, but I was too weary to go close his bedroom door. I couldn't call for help from my husband; he was gone on a business trip.

My eyes filled with tears of failure and self-pity. My high-need eighteen-month-old had obviously not read the same parenting books I had. If she had, she would know that after being fed, changed, rocked, and sung to for over an hour she was supposed to settle down and go to sleep. A tinge of nausea added to my discouragement. I was three months pregnant. How would I ever find the time or energy to parent a third child?

As if in rebuttal to my thoughts, the message of Psalm 127:3 came to my mind: *Children are a heritage, a reward, a blessing from the Lord.* I shook my head and almost laughed at what seemed to be a vast chasm between promise and reality. *Lord, would you spread this blessing on a little less thick?*

I supposed the writer of that Psalm had to have been a bachelor or perhaps a king with a queen and a harem of nursemaids to care for the constant demands of his children.

I understood the verse in one sense: I did experience precious moments of love, wonder, and fun with my children. But my spiritual life felt like it was slipping away. My devotional time had given way to naps and diaper washing whenever Christiana slept, which wasn't often. Sunday had shifted from a day of rest and worship to a stressful battle to get the children up and out the door. How did my relationship with God fit into the parenting picture beyond my constant prayers to be a better parent, to have more strength, wisdom, and love?

God answered me in a series of metaphors—rich picture descriptions of my relationship to him and his relationship to me. Jesus told us that when we enter the kingdom of God we are "born again." He also told us that we are to think of God as "Abba," Daddy. The prophet Isaiah referred to God as a mother who holds us on her lap. Jesus lamented over the people of Jerusalem, wanting to draw them to himself as a mother hen gathers her chicks. We are "children of God" and "children of Light." We are a part of "the family of God."

These phrases have become so common for many believers that the concepts they represent have lost their meaning. But God had a reason for talking about the Christian life in these terms. Even in a broken world where the family is far from perfect, God uses what we learn in our earthly families to give us a deeper understanding of what it means to be in relationship with him and each other.

Through raising our children, God is rearing us.

As I looked for God to apply this wonderful teaching tool, I began receiving God's blessing of lessons through parenting. I have learned more about what it means to call God my parent and what it means to be a child of God. I have learned from my children how to be a better parent and how to live a more abundant Christian life. My relationship with God has gained a richness and depth that it didn't have before my parenting years.

I believe that God intends the hectic years of parenting to be a soul-transforming time of growth in our lives of faith instead of a spiritually barren wilderness of exhaustion and frustration.

I invite you to read the stories recorded in these devotionals and to gain whatever insight God may have for you through them. I expect that although the names and the specifics will be different, many of the stories will resemble experiences you've had. It is my hope that sharing this perspective will connect you to the rich heritage God has given you through your children.

"Children *are* a blessing from the Lord!"

Day 1

LAPS IN LOVE

"Come to me, all you who are weary and burdened, and I will give you rest."

—Matthew 11:28

"You will nurse and be carried on her arm
and dandled on her knees.
As a mother comforts her child,
so will I comfort you."

—Isaiah 66:12–13

I glanced at the red numbers glaring at me from the microwave as I passed by on what felt like my millionth lap through the kitchen holding restless six-week-old Nathaniel.

Four in the morning.

Sigh.

I shifted Nathaniel to lay over my other arm in the airplane hold where the pressure of my arm against his tummy seemed to be the only thing keeping him comfortable.

I continued my laps—the kitchen, the foyer, the living room, the kitchen, the foyer, the living room. . . .

Nathaniel closed his eyes. His breathing evened. I slowed my march then tiptoed through the foyer. The recliner in the living room beckoned, and I eased myself onto the seat.

He wiggled; I held my breath. He settled again.

I leaned back in minute increments and began gently rocking. My weary eyes closed as my back touched the soft cushions.

Nathaniel whimpered and squirmed. Then, he let out an uncomfortable cry. *How does he know I sat down? I nursed him a half hour ago. He can't be hungry. I wonder if I ate something to give him gas?*

I turned him on his back and checked his diaper. It was dry.

I pumped his legs to rid him of gas. The cries continued.

I laid him across my knees and patted his back. My rocking quickened. The wailing increased.

What do you need?

Tears filled my eyes. I stopped my frantic rocking and took my baby and my frayed nerves on another lap. Immediately, his cries faded into whimpers. He hung over my arm, but I didn't pat his back. I just walked.

I felt empty and resentful—then, guilty and ashamed.

How can I feel resentful toward my own baby?

It's just that I've given him all I have to give, and he doesn't even seem to care. I wish someone would take care of me like I take care of him.

Tears streamed down my face as I paced around the loop, gently bouncing Nathaniel with the rhythm of my step.

Lord, help me!

"Come to me, all you who are weary and burdened, and I will give you rest."

I looked up to the gray ceiling and took a quivering breath.

All right, God. How?

The desire of my heart answered: I wish someone would take care of me like I take care of Nathaniel.

I am so weak. Please, Jesus, take care of me.

I closed my eyes and stood still. A spirit of calm wrapped around me as if the Spirit of Christ was standing next to me; his strong arm supporting me; his hand on my hand rubbing Nathaniel's back.

I walked. Held up, resting in God's loving care, I walked.

Reflections

Just like our children, we most need to be held by God during the stressful, painful, restless times. But often we let the draining demands of the moment crowd out our invitation for God's care. Spending time in God's nurturing presence and letting Jesus carry our burdens is not self-serving. Experiencing God's care as a reality in our lives helps us to better love our children, our spouses, and everyone with whom we come in contact.

Prayer

Dear God, even though I'm a parent, I'm still your child, and I need your loving care. Help me to realize that you call me to come to you, and you long to bless me just as you did the little children in the Bible. Hide me under your wing when I'm hurting and restless. Let me rest in your arms when I'm weary. It's wonderful to know that even when I'm parenting my children, you're always there as a resting place, a loving parent for me. Amen.

 RGANIC PARENTING

Let us not become weary in doing good, for at the proper time
we will reap a harvest if we do not give up.

—Galatians 6:9

The early spring sun warmed my violet sweatshirt as two-year-old Nathaniel knelt next to me on the picnic table clutching a package of nasturtium seeds. I hefted a bag of potting soil onto the table and filled an empty egg carton with the loamy soil.

"Are you ready with the seeds?"

Nathaniel's mass of golden curls bobbed up and down. He twisted the package trying to rip it open.

"Do you need some help?"

"No."

Nathaniel was a boy of few words.

A shower of seeds scattered onto the table and spilled into the grass. He looked up with wide eyes and open mouth.

I smiled. "It's all right. Make a hole with your finger, and I'll put in a seed."

Nathaniel pushed his chubby index finger into each cup. I gathered up the tan, wrinkled spheres and placed one into each hole.

"Put some dirt over each seed, and then we'll water them."

Nathaniel scooped up handfuls of soil and created a mountainous landscape atop the egg carton.

I brushed the excess soil onto the ground and smoothed the picture on the wrinkled package.

"This is what they will look like in a few weeks."

Nathaniel took the package from me and nodded.

I searched out a Popsicle stick and stood the envelope of promise in one of the cups. The empty package displayed a colorful array of orange, yellow, and maroon blossoms.

Nathaniel was delighted with our diminutive windowsill garden.

The next day, Nathaniel climbed up on the booth in our kitchen; he studied the dirt-filled cups.

"Flowers?"

"Not yet. It will be ten days." I held up both hands. "This many sleep times."

Nathaniel hopped down.

The next day, he climbed up on the booth again to examine the dirt-filled egg carton.

I repeated my explanation; he jumped down.

The third day, he didn't climb up to see. I asked if he would like to help water the seeds. This was a hit (any activity involving water always interested him). Over the next several days, he occasionally glanced at the egg carton but didn't bother to climb up to see.

When the little plants emerged—ten days later—Nathaniel was very pleased. During his renewed routine of daily inspections, I saw his eyes shift back and forth comparing the tender shoots and tiny round leaves with the vibrant blossoms and rich foliage in the picture. But, after a week of inspections, he refused to check anymore.

When the time was right, I transplanted the nasturtiums into the border along our front walk. Four weeks later, they blossomed.

I knelt next to Nathaniel on the walk.

"Do you like the flowers we planted?"

He nodded tentatively but looked away.

I don't think Nathaniel associated the colorful flowers with the tiny wrinkled seeds we buried in the egg cartons weeks earlier. With the limited perspective of his twenty-four-months-of-life experience, Nathaniel couldn't comprehend the connection.

Reflections

As we try to plant God's seeds of love and truth in our children's lives, we often become impatient to see immediate results. When we have faith that God is at work in our children's lives, we can take our hands off areas where we have faithfully planted seeds, knowing the Holy Spirit is operating, perhaps in ways we cannot see or comprehend.

Prayer

Dear God, help me to have your eternal perspective on time, enabling me to flourish in the art of organic parenting. Strengthen my faith in the connection between planting seeds and seeing blossoms. Help me not to despair when I don't see immediate results in the outward actions of my children. Hold my will steady when I'm tempted to neglect my children in order to put my energies into tasks that give instantaneous reward for my efforts. Amen.

EARNING TO CLIMB

*For he will command his angels concerning you
to guard you in all your ways.*

—Psalm 91:11

"Good-bye."

I hung up the phone. Through the picture window, I could see Nathaniel swaying back and forth, belly down on the swing. I smiled at his apparent fascination with the dusty ground beneath him. The yard was fenced, so my two-and-a-half-year-old was confined and safe from wandering away.

I walked into the kitchen to put the phone away and spied a pillow peeking out from under the edge of the table where I suspected Nathaniel had been playing fort. While returning the pillow to the living room couch, I glanced out the window.

Nathaniel wasn't on the swing.

Usually, he insisted that I help him climb the ladder to the wooden fort. The ladder was attached to the side of the fort opposite the slide. The sides of the ladder extended above the platform floor of the fort but did not offer any easy handles for transferring from the ladder to the safety of the walled platform.

Nathaniel was perched near the top of the ladder, hanging on to the wooden side rails, motionless. A ripple of anxiety ran through my gut. I started to open the window and call to him to hold on until I got there.

Nathaniel moved from his frozen stance. Holding on with one arm, he lunged toward the wall of the fort with the opposite hand. He missed his target, swung back, and grabbed the ladder again.

I took in a quick breath and fumbled frantically with the stubborn latch.

Wait and watch, said an inner voice.

I paused.

Moms are always too protective of firstborns.

I let go of the latch and stared at Nathaniel, as if trying to hold him up with my anxious gaze. The distance to the ground wasn't more than a few feet; he was holding on tightly.

Nathaniel reached up higher and lifted first one foot and then the other to the next highest rung. Now his hands were at the top of the rail extensions, his feet almost level with the floor of the fort. Again he gripped one side rail and lunged for the wall of the fort with his free hand.

He had it!

I bit my lower lip.

He stepped onto the platform and shifted his weight forward and back, forward and back, forward and—into the fort!

I exhaled and hurried to the backyard.

Nathaniel climbed down and ran toward me, a proud grin lighting up his face. He pointed to the ladder and mumbled an unintelligible account of his great feat. I didn't need an interpreter.

"You climbed the ladder all by yourself?"

His head bobbed up and down like a bouncing ball.

"That's terrific!"

I stooped down and he flung his arms around my neck, then jerked away and ran back to the ladder.

I wasn't needed as ladder monitor anymore. I'd worked my way out of a job, and it wasn't hard.

I just had to wait.

Reflections

Sometimes we wonder where God is when we are growing in our faith and stretching our spiritual abilities. In those times, could it be that God is encouraging us to trust and have faith in his love as a fact even if we don't feel his immediate presence? The Bible tells us that hope is "the evidence of things not seen" (Heb. 11:1 KJV). Let us resolve to hope in God as our loving parent who is always watching over us even when we don't see him there.

Prayer

Dear God, sometimes when you wait and don't run to my rescue, I wonder if you care. Help me to realize that you are always watching. Help me to keep on trying when I am learning a new task in your service or working on a difficult challenge in my personal growth. Help me to trust you to be there when I am in real need. Make me willing to take the risks to try new things in order to grow and develop as your child.

I remember the many times I have run into your loving, affirming arms to share the joy of growth and accomplishment. Thank you for always being there when I need you—even in times when I most need you to watch and wait. Amen.

 SPACE OF MY OWN

"For my thoughts are not your thoughts,
neither are your ways my ways,"
declares the LORD.

—Isaiah 55:8

"If anyone loves me, he will obey my teaching. My Father will
love him, and we will come to him and make our home with
him."

—John 14:23

The LORD is my shepherd, I shall lack nothing.
He makes me lie down in green pastures,
he leads me beside quiet waters,
he restores my soul.
He guides me in paths of righteousness
for his name's sake.

—Psalm 23:1–3

Four forty-five, time to pick up Don from work. I set down the latest *National Geographic* and watched my three-year-old collecting rocks from our gravel drive. Nathaniel squatted above the treasure trove of crushed quarry and examined each stone as if intent on discovering a hidden diamond in their midst.

"Nathaniel, it's time to go get Papa."

Nathaniel looked up. His straight-lined lips and slightly squinted eyes signaled the beginning of a refusal. Before the clash became overt, requiring follow-through consequences, I added, "We can go now, or we can go in five minutes."

"In fi' minute."

He resumed his search.

I tried to give Nathaniel as many choices as I could. Most days I offered him two outfits, two vegetables, two games, two coloring books . . . two of whatever. He was catching on though; recently, he had been countering with a third option.

His inborn sense of preference fascinated me. Why yellow and red clothes instead of the traditional little boy blue? Why pea soup and salmon cakes instead of the all-time-kid-favorite macaroni and cheese? At least if he kept up his internal sense of self, I wouldn't have to worry about negative peer pressure influences.

I affirmed his tastes within the boundaries of health, resources, and safety.

Safety.

Oh yes, the always-required toddler car seat. We had just purchased a new one for our growing firstborn. I looked at my watch and frowned.

"It's time to go, Nathaniel."

He glanced at me and then went back to his stone study.

I stood up and stepped toward him. "It's been five minutes, Son. Don't you want to see Papa?"

He stood up.

Good.

I scooped him up in my arms, marched into the house, grabbed my purse, then hummed and danced Nathaniel out to the car. I opened the back door of the Honda and swung Nathaniel into the waiting apparatus.

"No!" He straight-armed the padded shield. Why couldn't he let it go peacefully even one time?

"Nathaniel, you've got to ride in your car seat so you will be safe. Please let go."

His bottom lip folded under the puffy upper one.

"Nathaniel, let go of the seat, or you'll have consequences."

He didn't budge.

"I will have to restrain your hands if you disobey with them."

He flexed his elbows; I fastened the seat. But as soon as he heard the "click" of the latch, he exploded like a caged monkey. He leaned hard to the side, pulling and pushing around the red release button.

"Let me out!"

I gathered his wrists and held them in front of him in a thumb-and-fingers pillory. "No, Nathaniel. You must stay in your seat or you could get hurt very badly. Mommy doesn't want you to get hurt."

He twisted and pulled at his captive wrists as if I had been speaking to him in a foreign language. It was a kind of foreign language to him, an adult language with adult ideas.

Having decided that his turning fury couldn't loosen him, he held his clenched fists still. He began swinging his feet against the front seat.

"Do I need to restrain you longer, or are you ready to behave?"

He stopped kicking and nodded his head.

"Look at me, Nathaniel. Are you ready to behave?"

He jerked his back against the seat and gazed at me with reluctant submission.

"Yes."

I released him; he jerked his hands behind the bolster. I shut the door and climbed in the front seat. I located Nathaniel in the rearview mirror, popped a kid song tape in the cassette player, and pulled out of the driveway.

Halfway down Eighth Street, I heard the rattling of the car seat release latch. I glanced at Nathaniel. His head was no longer located in the upright position but was hunched over the latch side of his seat.

"Nathaniel, leave that alone!"

"Nathaniel, there will be consequences!"

"Click." I watched in dismay as the safety bar flung open. Adrenaline flooded my system. I spied an open curb on the busy street and swerved into the space. My heart pounded. A safe landing. *Thank you, Lord!*

Time to attend to my high-energy, strong-willed—foolish— son. We would be late picking up Don.

Reflections

At times we all have trouble obeying God's rules. Perhaps no big sin category comes to mind, but think of Christ's admonitions concerning the attitudes of the heart. How easy it is to nurse a secret grudge or to share a word of gossip in the guise of a prayer request. Sometimes we discount the importance of certain biblical commands because we do not understand the reason behind the rule. Remember that God is our designer and creator with the loving heart of a perfect parent. When we truly believe God has our best eternal interests and safety in mind, we can let go of our rebellious spirit and trust his Word.

Prayer

Dear God, you give me many choices because you are love and love requires choice. You have also given me rules to protect me from destruction and guidelines that lead me to abundant life. Help me to realize that in comparison to you, I am but a babe in spirit, limited in my understanding. Let my choices be within my love for you and your love for me, that my life may be held safely in your everlasting way. Amen.

THE PUZZLE OF MY LIFE

Trust in the LORD *with all your heart*
and lean not on your own understanding;
in all your ways acknowledge him,
and he will make your paths straight.

—Proverbs 3:5–6

I dumped the twenty-five pieces of the cute puppy-in-the-grass puzzle onto the table. Nathaniel pushed his hands into the pile, pulled out a couple of tan, furry, puppy pieces and tried to fit a rounded knob into a notch. At age four, he had mastered all of the frame puzzles in the house, and I thought he would enjoy the challenge of a real puzzle.

"First you look for all the pieces with a straight edge." I ran my finger along the smooth side of an edge piece.

"I want to make the puppy."

"But honey, you have to put the outside together first to make a frame for the puzzle. Then, you can fill it in with the picture of the puppy. It's easier that way."

Nathaniel twisted one side of his mouth up into an all-right-if-you-say-so-but-I'm-not-convinced expression.

"Let's put the edge pieces over here and the rest of the pieces back in the box for now."

I pulled out of the pile a couple of pieces with grassy flowered background and tossed them into the box. Nathaniel fingered the picture fragments, turning them over and pushing them around into a single layer. He studied the design on each one before depositing it in the box or placing it in the straight edge collection.

"Why?" he asked.

"Why what?"

"Why's it better?"

"Well . . . because you have a frame, and it gives you a place to start. That's the way I've always done it."

"But, I want the puppy."

Nathaniel picked up two tan cardboard segments, one with the puppy's eye and one with its nose, and fit the knob into the notch.

"See."

I chuckled. "Good for you. But I think you'll find it a bit harder when you get the obvious parts like the face done."

Nathaniel shrugged. He laid his two piece section aside and started sorting again. His procedure was not the rapid, straight-edge-radar arranging like mine. He scrutinized the partial design of each piece before placing it in one of the mom-designated categories.

After a few silent seconds, he picked up a notched and knobby piece and held it next to his one-eyed puppy face. He rotated it in a couple of 360° spins. Then, he clicked it into place, giving his puppy a second eye and the beginning of a floppy ear.

"Wow, you're pretty good at this, Nathaniel."

He smiled.

"You know when I was growing up, seven of us girls in my neighborhood used to get together in the summers and do jigsaw puzzles with a couple thousand pieces. We always made the outside frame first. Sometimes it took us two or three passes sorting through the pieces to find all of the edges."

I wonder if we weren't wasting our time.

Nathaniel nodded. He fit another piece in place. The crown of the puppy's head curved in completion.

"We used to say 'click' whenever we got a piece to let everyone else know. It was sort of fun because it made you feel like you were getting somewhere, hearing all those 'clicks' around the table. Do you want to do that?"

"Click."

"That's right."

"No, I got a piece."

He pointed proudly to where another ear had materialized on the puppy.

"That's great."

I picked up the last piece to sort. Notches and knobs. I started to toss it in the box and then noticed the image: a lolling pink tongue poking from the velvet jowls of a puppy face. It wasn't an edge piece, but—I tossed the piece onto the table in front of Nathaniel.

"Here."

"Thanks. Click."

The charming face stared out at us as if in thanksgiving. We would enjoy working on the rest of the puzzle with the soulful gaze of the puppy to cheer us on.

"I tell you what. Why don't I work on the frame, and you can go back through the other pieces to finish the puppy."

Reflections

The rules governing our spiritual lives often go beyond the guidelines of Scripture. In our church communities and in the popular culture, even in our families, we learn unspoken rules. Music styles, dress codes, or a certain order to doing things are examples of behaviors that have a basis in human reason. Usually these ways of doing things are not evil in themselves. But when they become a means of control or when they take precedence over the leading of God's Spirit, they become crippling, limiting God's creative work in our lives and in the church.

Prayer

Dear God, I like order and control in my life. I like to know what all the possible pieces are. I like the security of a frame telling me the limits of what I might experience and expect. But I don't have a box top to show me what the final picture of my life will look like. Help me to look to you as my master puzzle worker. Help me to contemplate the content of each experience, each day, each relationship, and not instantly categorize my life, throwing aside the pieces that I can't fit into the portrait I have in mind. Help me to open my hand to receive whatever pieces you give me, placing each one reverently into the puzzle of my life, revealing the joyful picture you are eternally creating in me. Amen.

DISCONNECTED FROM THE STEM

"I am the vine; you are the branches. If a man remains in me and I in him, he will bear much fruit; apart from me you can do nothing. If anyone does not remain in me, he is like a branch that is thrown away and withers."

—John 15:5–6

Nathaniel strolled down the sidewalk in front of me toward the front door. Sweat trickled down my back as I carried two bags of groceries from our oven-baked compact car. Four-year-old Nathaniel stopped to examine an ant crossing the walk.

"Honey, please hurry. Mommy's carrying heavy bags."

He skipped on a few feet and then sighted the patch of giant columbine. He grabbed a stem, just below one of the delicate violet and yellow blossoms.

"Nathaniel, please don't pick those flowers."

I crowded him away from my favorite perennials with my hip. He stumbled forward and looked at me with surprise.

"You may pick the dandelions and the violets and clover in the yard, but let's leave these flowers to grow so we can enjoy them longer."

"Why?"

Our budding scientist desired to understand his world, and

if he didn't think my answers were sufficient, he often used the experimental method to satisfy his curiosity. So, I tried to explain—in self-defense.

"If you pick the flowers, they will die. But if you leave them here, they will be stay pretty."

"Why?"

"Because they need the nourishment and water that they get from the soil through their stems."

He mumbled something about the dandelions and violets.

"Nathaniel, the dandelions and violets are pretty when you bring them to me, but you don't see them after they wilt because Mommy throws them out. Please, just don't pick these flowers. I planted them so we could enjoy them when we walk on the sidewalk."

I scooted him ahead of me into the house.

A couple of days later, I was picking up sticks in the front yard when Nathaniel brought me a bouquet of giant columbine.

"Oh, Nathaniel!"

"See, Mom, they are *too* pretty!"

"Oh, Nathaniel."

My anger dissolved into a weary sigh.

"They will be pretty for a little while, but then they will die. Come on. Let's go put them in some water."

Nathaniel took his time-out for disobeying, and a couple of days later I made sure he helped me throw the dead flowers away.

Reflections

Jesus told us that when we are disconnected from him, we can do nothing of eternal worth. Abiding in Christ is a process and a relationship.

Abiding indicates that we know Jesus loves us. It also suggests that we know him and trust him to be a secure place to live. Getting to know Jesus through reading the Gospels can help us shift from abiding in ourselves, in our worries, and in our knowledge, to abiding in him.

Worshiping with believers, hearing others' stories about Jesus' faithfulness, and asking Jesus to make us aware of his working in our lives can also move us into an abiding relationship with the source of our spiritual life.

Prayer

Dear God, help me to stay connected to you every day so that I can draw nourishment and refreshment for my soul from your living water. When I let the everyday demands of life pluck me from your garden, I may appear for a short time to flourish without you, but slowly my heart wilts. Guard me from this destructive deception of self-sufficiency, and keep me rooted in you. You are the life source of my soul. You are joy and peace, goodness and hope, strength and faith. Amen.

LOVE AND HAMMERS

There is no fear in love. But perfect love drives out fear.

—1 John 4:18

The dry wood of the laden drawer screeched its protest as Don wrenched it open in uneven jerks. The old dresser we had put in the garage served as a storage place for an assortment of little-used tools and odd-shaped hardware.

Our four-year-old son squatted a few feet away next to his new bicycle and training wheels, waiting his father's return.

"Hey, Nathaniel, come here."

Nathaniel scooted to Don's side. He leaned over his father's knee and peered into the unrecognizable collection of dust-dulled steel and grip-carved wooden dowels. From the morass of rods and curves, Don pulled out a hammer. He tenderly rubbed the well-worn oak handle and polished up the steel head. He balanced the antique tool across his open palms.

"Nathaniel, do you know whose hammer this is?"

Nathaniel shook his head.

Don pointed to the flat side of the steel head. A hint of red highlighted the letters J. G. B.

"Those initials belong to your great grandfather, Jacob Gordon Boggs. This hammer belonged to him a long time ago when he worked in the sawmill in West Virginia."

Nathaniel traced the letters, the soft pink of his finger contrasting with the hard, dark surface.

"When your grandpa, John Gordon Boggs, became a man, his father, Jacob, gave him this hammer. When I became a man, Grandpa gave this hammer to me. My name is Donald Gordon Boggs, and your name is Nathaniel Gordon Boggs. When you become a man, I will give this hammer to you. Would you like that?"

Nathaniel nodded.

"And then someday, if you have a son, you can give this hammer to him. If he has a son, he can pass down the hammer again."

Nathaniel wrapped his fingers around the handle and lifted. The heavy tool headed for the floor. Don caught the weighty heirloom in his hands. Nathaniel leaned against Don's leg. He chewed his lower lip and swayed.

"Papa, will you be here when I give it to my son?"

"Um—why, yes, Nathaniel, I'll probably be alive then. But perhaps not when your son gives the hammer to *his* son."

Nathaniel placed his tender, stubby fingers on the veined, tanned hand of his father. He leaned forward and his eyebrows drew together studying Don's face. With serene intensity, he concluded his examination.

"I will miss you when you are gone, Papa."

Don's eyes reddened. He cleared his throat and looked away.

"I will miss you, too, Nathaniel."

Reflections

One of the incredible blessings of being a Christian is that we no longer need to fear death! Yet our feelings do not always match what we want to believe. Especially for those who have suffered loss or felt abandoned at a young age, or for those who have unresolved issues with the ones who have died or left them, thoughts about death can bring up deep feelings of pain and anxiety.

God doesn't want us to pretend that we have it all together

when we are, in reality, hurting or afraid. Instead, God invites us to bring our feelings and thoughts into the light of love to be gently transformed into faith and hope. Then we can sense God's protective and forever love surrounding us and tenderly embracing us with the promise of eternal life.

*P*r a y e r

Dear God, help me to have faith in your promise of eternal life and peace in your presence now and forever. May I live in the heritage of your eternal perspective. May my steady gaze in the face of passing from this life leave my children with a calm and constant hope of your abiding presence for them and for all generations to come. Amen.

ESUS OFF THE CROSS

*"The LORD does not look at the things man looks at. Man looks
at the outward appearance, but the LORD looks at the heart."*
—1 Samuel 16:7

Don walked into the bedroom and shuffled through the papers, pens, and end of the day deposits accumulated on his
dresser. The latest issue of *Broadcasting Magazine* fell to the
floor along with yesterday's pocket change.

"Tamara, do you know where my crucifix is?"

A couple of months earlier, Don had purchased a necklace
with a crucifix to wear under his clothes as a private reminder
of the precious gift our Savior gave to us in his death. Our
Protestant tradition preferred displaying the empty cross, symbolizing the risen Christ, and seldom gave any visual icon for
meditation on Christ's sacrifice.

"I thought I left it on the bathroom counter last night, but I
can't find it anywhere," Don said.

"I don't know. Did you check by the bed?"

"Yes. That's one of the first places I looked."

"Christiana!" Nathaniel's angry howl from the children's
bedroom cued my exit.

Christiana, a mildly autistic child of three, frequently
screamed, hit, pinched, and scratched to communicate dis-
pleasure. Telling her to "use her words" was like telling a snake

to walk—the ability just wasn't there. I knew that her delay in speech development contributed to her physical expressions of frustration, but her behavior was still unacceptable.

I was weary of the constant need to discipline her. Any negative intervention heightened her angry feelings resulting in attacks against toys and other household items; most didn't survive without major damage. Nothing valuable or fragile could be safely left within her reach.

Christiana uttered a frustrated squeal as I walked into their room.

"What's going on?"

Christiana sat on the floor next to the bed rubbing her eyes and pointing to Nathaniel. "Mine!"

Nathaniel opened his hand to show me the object of controversy. "Look what Christiana did!"

A dull silver chain looped from Nathaniel's fingers. In his palm lay a plain pewter cross. Three minute holes punctuated the cross where once had been fastened the image of the crucified Christ.

"Oh, Christiana," I sighed, lamenting the loss of the special symbol. "You'll have to take a time-out on the couch."

I took the cross and chain from Nathaniel and grasped Christiana's arm to lead her to the living room. My tone shifted from tender grief to weary tension. "You mustn't touch other people's things."

Christiana pulled away and plopped back down on the floor. "No!"

Don walked into the room. I handed him the remains. "Sorry."

One side of Don's brow furrowed. "Where's Jesus?" he asked.

I shook my head. "Who knows? Christiana, come right now or there will be further consequences. It will only be for a few minutes if you come now."

Christiana began sobbing as if a few minutes on the couch meant a lifetime in a dungeon. I picked her up. She wiggled and kicked, but I managed to get her on the couch.

"Papa . . . But, Mommy . . . But, Mommy . . ."

"But what, Christiana? You have got to stop destroying things. If you are angry about something, you need to try to use your words or hit a pillow or your bed, something you can't hurt. You mustn't tear things up."

"But, Mommy . . ."

She sounded so sad. A repentant Christiana was unusual. I decided I would make this a thirty-second time-out if she continued to cooperate. "Are you sorry you broke Papa's necklace?"

She nodded. "But, Mommy . . ." She opened her hand and held out a tiny metallic form. "Jesus."

"Thank you, Christiana. You stay here and think about not breaking things when you're angry, and it will only be a little while."

I took the figure and turned to go. I glanced down at the diminutive pewter body with its loin cloth and crown of thorns. *Jesus.*

Christiana had probably never seen a cross with Christ on it before. I sat down next to her. "Christiana, why did you break Papa's necklace?"

She pointed to the Christ image. "Jesus, off."

"You wanted Jesus off the cross?"

The corners of her mouth twitched upward, and she nodded.

I looked again at the figure of Jesus, resurrected this time by the will of a three-year-old—an act of love—mistaken.

Reflections

As humans, we naturally focus on behaviors more than motivations, both in our children and ourselves. All of us have had experiences where our good intentions have been mistaken or where our good behaviors have masked inward bitterness. Jesus taught that the intent of our hearts is much more important than outward appearances when we follow in God's way. How precious that God, our perfect parent, listens to our hearts.

P r a y e r

Dear God, help me to see with your eyes. Help me to listen to hearts as you do. When you walked with fragile human beings on this earth, you looked through their sinful actions and had compassion on them, knowing their longings and shortcomings. Give me the insight to judge between intentional acts of rebellion in my children and wrong acts based on ignorance, inability, or thoughtlessness. You see my actions and know my heart, and you judge me with justice, mercy, and compassion. May I give to others that which I have received from you. Amen.

Day 9

JESUS IN TRACTION

Christ Jesus:
Who, being in very nature God,
  did not consider equality with God something to be
  grasped,
but made himself nothing,
  taking the very nature of a servant,
  being made in human likeness.
And being found in appearance as a man,
  he humbled himself
  and became obedient to death—even death on a cross!
Therefore God exalted him to the highest place
  and gave him the name that is above every name,
that at the name of Jesus every knee should bow,
  in heaven and on earth and under the earth,
and every tongue confess that Jesus Christ is Lord,
  to the glory of God the Father.
                                                    —Philippians 2:5–11

"I tell you the truth, anyone who has faith in me will do what
I have been doing. . . . And I will do whatever you ask in my
name, so that the Son may bring glory to the Father."
                                                    —John 14:12–13

"Your child will be in the hospital for at least four weeks."
I thought I had heard the doctor wrong. "What do you

46

mean?" I asked to break the awkward stupidity of my stunned silence.

"She has a spiral fracture of the left femur and will require surgery today to place a pin through the lower end of the bone. She will need to remain in the hospital in traction for at least four weeks for the bone to mend properly. I will see her in surgery at one o'clock. Someone from pediatrics will be with you shortly to take her up to her room."

I nodded.

The doctor strode away in brisk confidence, unaware that his precise, penetrating missile of words had wreaked devastation on my life. Three-year-old Christiana lay peacefully on the gurney beside me and smiled. "Honey, it looks like you're going to get to stay in the hospital for a while," I said. My heart ached as I looked into her trusting eyes.

"Mommy, are you going to stay?"

"Yes, Mommy is staying."

My mind raced home to my seven-year-old Nathaniel and nine-month-old Hannah—so many details to work out.

The day was stressed with IV needles and panicked screams from Christiana as they wheeled her away from me into surgery. At least the nurses let me into the recovery room before she awoke. It gave me time to weep at the sight of the gruesome metal pin protruding from above her left knee. A sling supported her lower leg, and her bottom was lifted an inch off the bed by the weights hanging from the pulleys that kept tension on the pin. Her left femur was straight, but her body was contorted.

I sniffed back my tears and stroked her hair as her eyes fluttered open.

"Mommy?" she mumbled and then drifted back to sleep.

"The doctor has prescribed pain killers for her," the nurse said, her fingers on Christiana's pulse, her eyes on her watch. "The first several days they usually have a fair amount of pain, and then most children do very well."

Two o'clock the next morning, the nurse's promise of lessening pain in the coming days shimmered through my thoughts like an oasis on the horizon. Standing at Christiana's bedside, I had been trudging through the dehydrating desert of watching one I love suffer. For the past eight hours, helplessness had drained me of all my energy and encouraging words.

Even with the pain medication, Christiana had slept only in twenty-minute intervals, waking and calling for me to come and "make it stop hurting." My hands cramped from massaging the knotted muscles of her back. My neck throbbed from hours spent half-bent over her hospital bed, holding her sweaty hand, rubbing, stroking, soothing her spasmodic muscles. My head nodded.

"Mommy!" Christiana cried.

I jerked back to attention. *Help us, Lord.* My prayers had shortened as the day had worn on.

Sing. The answer came. Perhaps singing would help me stay awake and take Christiana's mind off the pain.

"Michael row your boat ashore, Halleluia. Michael, row your boat ashore—"

"No, Mommy."

Frustration surged through me; tears filled my eyes. Was there nothing I could do?

"Jesus songs, Mommy. Jesus songs."

"Okay, Honey. . . . Jesus loves me, this I know, . . ." My tears dripped onto her bed. "For the Bible tells me so. Little ones to him belong, . . ." My voice trembled. "They are weak, but he is strong. Yes, Jesus loves me. . . ."

Christiana's monotone joined me. "Yes, Jesus loves me. Yes, Jesus loves me. The Bible tells me so."

I rested my head on my arms folded against her bed. A cleansing peace calmed my frazzled nerves.

"More Jesus songs."

I lifted my face to meet her gaze with a weary smile. "Jesus,

Jesus, Jesus in the morning, Jesus at the noontime. Jesus, Jesus, Jesus when the sun goes down."

More songs with Jesus' name came to my mind. I sang in a hoarse whisper from my dry, tear-soaked throat, but Christiana didn't mind. I rubbed her back, a renewed spirit of love strengthening my touch. Her squirming against the pull of the weights lessened; she relaxed.

I sang Bill and Gloria Gaither's "There's Something About That Name" to the calmed rhythm of her slumbering breath.

"Jesus, Jesus, Jesus. There's just something about that name. . . ."*

Reflections

The name of Jesus, the person of the living Christ, can season all of our moments, especially our stressful times, with the love, rest, peace, and power God has given us through the wonderful name of Jesus. Perhaps today can be a Jesus song day for you.

Prayer

Dear God, thank you for Jesus. Often I go through my day defended in my own strength against the demands and pressures and hurts of life. But, under my self-sufficient fortress, I sometimes feel so fragile. Through your incarnational life in Jesus, I know you understand me in all my humanity. Through Jesus' name, I have access to you, to your love and strength and peace. How wonder-filled I am that I can come to you! Please bring to my heart and mind songs that praise the precious name of Jesus. Amen.

---

* "There's Something About That Name," William J. Gaither, © 1970, William J. Gaither. Used by permission.

"I DON'T WANT YOU TO MISS ME"

"Then the righteous will answer him, 'Lord, when did we see you hungry and feed you, or thirsty and give you something to drink? When did we see you . . . needing clothes and clothe you? When did we see you sick . . . and go to visit you?'

"The King will reply, 'I tell you the truth, whatever you did for one of the least of these [children] of mine, you did for me.'"

—Matthew 25:37–40

"If anyone gives a cup of cold water to one of these little ones because he is my disciple, I tell you the truth, he will certainly not lose his reward."

—Matthew 10:42

I hurried down the hall toward the counter full of dirty dishes and the stack of medical bills waiting for me to sort and pay.

"Maw-meee," Christiana called from her bedroom.

I stopped and took a deep breath to release the fountain of frustration welling up inside me. Christiana had been home from the hospital and out of her body cast for two months. Her leg had healed fine, but we had not been able to get her back to her pre-hospital, pre-broken-leg bedtime routine.

"What does she want?" Don asked.

"I don't know." I walked into the living room. "I read her and Hannah a story, got her a drink, and rubbed her back. The dishes need to be done, and I have medical insurance stuff to work on."

Don closed his book. "Which would you like me to do? Dishes or Christiana?"

"I'll do dishes." A little detached dish work to wind down from the day's caregiving would be nice.

Don placed his copy of *Men in Space* on the side table and gave me a wish-me-luck smile.

"Thanks, Honey." I headed to the kitchen.

"I want Mommy." The defensive anxiety in Christiana's tone made my stomach tense in anticipation of what I imagined would be a war of the wills, complete with battle cries and high decibel carnage. Don was very good with her, very loving, but firm and unbending once he issued an edict. But I wasn't emotionally up to hearing her cry this evening. I slid the dinner plate back into the sink and hurried toward Christiana's room.

"It's all right." I interrupted Don's iron-clad "It's time to go to sleep now" speech.

"What do you need, Christiana?" I asked.

Christiana sniffed back the beginnings of her protest at what she perceived as my neglect to respond to her call.

"She'll be fine," Don said.

"I know, but . . ."

Don shook his head but stood up to relinquish his good-night position on the edge of the bed. "I'll go do dishes."

I sat down. "What do you need, Christiana?" I was hoping to accomplish a peaceful strategic withdrawal after a hug and a kiss.

"Mommy, lie down with me. I don't want you to miss me."

"You mean, *you* don't want to miss *me*."

She nodded the whatever-you-say nod. A nudge by the Holy

Spirit inside of me confronted my condescending correction of Christiana's speech. She didn't want *me* to miss *her.*

I pulled her up into my arms and wrapped the covers around us both. Her eyes held me with a fullness of gratitude, letting me know I was needed and loved. The effort it took to hold her was so little. The dishes and bills faded away behind her sleepy grin.

I kissed her forehead. "I love you, Christiana. I don't want to miss you either."

Reflections

As parents, we do need to set limits and boundaries regarding our availability to come at every beck and call of our children. Yet, there are times when it is easy to shut down sensitivity to the genuine needs of our children in response to our own busyness. When we let God open our hearts to his discerning Spirit, we can learn a sensitivity that carries over into all the relationships of our lives.

Prayer

Dear God, help me not to miss my children. In the midst of the busy details of life, help me to discern when I need to lay the temporal demands of living aside and focus on an eternal moment with one of them. Then, as they grow toward you, their heavenly parent, help them to remember our times of being together as a model of how important it is to sometimes put away things that will pass away in order to seek eternal moments with you. For you always come when your children call, "I don't want you to miss me!" Amen.

"MY NAME IS NATHANIEL BOGGS"

Those who are lead by the Spirit of God are [children] of God. For you did not receive a spirit that makes you a slave again to fear, but you received the Spirit of [an heir]. And by him we cry, "Abba, Father." The Spirit himself testifies with our spirit that we are God's children.

—Romans 8:14–16

I entered the gymnasium where the kids were playing in hopes of catching a glimpse of my son in the midst of the game. The pit of my stomach fluttered like a bird in a chimney flue, and my hands were clammy and cold. I chastised myself for being such a typical parent and hoped my outward appearance was calm and reassuring.

More than a hundred and fifty kids were playing on that gym floor and the quiet was unnerving—yes, the quiet. Only the slapping of hands on clock timers and the tapping rhythm of resin kings and queens broke the silence of the scholastic chess competition. Long lines of tables surrounded by focused young faces created an atmosphere of competitive fervor. No referee's whistle or lighted board let me know how well the kids were playing; grins and grimaces told the score.

I inched my way around the perimeter of the gym toward

Nathaniel at board 12. I was careful not to get too close. I didn't want to disrupt his focus. I found him standing over his board, studying the position of his pieces from above.

His move. His opponent's move. His move. His opponent's move. Then, the other boy stood; they shook hands. It was all over.

Nathaniel rolled up his vinyl board, and they put the pieces in his bag. They walked over to the scoring table and reported the results. I fidgeted near the door.

I smiled as Nathaniel came out. His face was expressionless. "So, how'd it go?"

"I won."

"That's great! That puts you 3 and 0."

"I guess so."

"What's wrong?"

"Where's Papa?"

At age seven, this was Nathaniel's second scholastic chess tournament. I had come along with our daughters, alternating with Don throughout the day to watch his games. But evidently, playing chess had become a father and son thing.

"Papa's with the girls in the lunch room."

We walked down the noisy hall to the cafeteria, where practice games and grab-when-you-can lunches were spread over the tables. Christiana and Hannah hugged me as if I had been gone all day instead of forty-five minutes.

"Papa, I won. Who do I play now?"

"I don't know, son. We'll have to wait and see when they post the next round. What's wrong?"

"I don't know. . . . I might have to play someone really good."

"You just play your best and don't worry about it. Remember, 'When you lose, you learn.'"

Nathaniel managed a half grin.

"Postings for round four are up," the tournament director called.

Round four found Nathaniel sitting at the number one

board across from the boy who was ranked first in the tournament. Before Nathaniel arrived, the boy had set up his expensive, weighted chess pieces and his sleek, digital game clock. He picked up his pencil and began filling out his notation pad, where he would record all the moves of the game. Nathaniel hadn't yet learned how to take notation and sat with his hands in his lap.

"So," Nathaniel's opponent asked, "what's your rating?" The boy stared at Nathaniel, his head cocked to the side in birdlike examination. He waited for Nathaniel to tell him the U.S. Chess Federation rating number indicating Nathaniel's ability level.

Nathaniel shifted in his seat and returned the boy's gaze. "I don't have a rating . . . but my name is Nathaniel Boggs."

An hour later, Nathaniel shook the boy's hand, reported to the scoring table, and walked out into the hallway.

"How did it go?" Don asked.

"I lost."

Don put a comforting arm around Nathaniel's shoulder. Nathaniel pulled away a bit and smiled. "It's okay."

I looked at the peaceful expression on his face. He was right. Win or lose, Nathaniel Boggs was okay.

Reflections

Being God's child is at the center of our identity as Christians. Anything else we base our identity and worth on, such as our abilities, our looks, our strengths, our children, or our connections, are shaky foundations that we may someday lose. Be assured that each of us *is* a precious child of God. No matter what challenges or circumstances we face, even when we lose by the world's standards, God stands by us and cheers us on.

P r a y e r

Dear God, when the world asks for my credentials of worth, may I know who I am and answer with confidence. Help me to know that in the game of life, often, losing gives me an opportunity to learn. Help me to remember that my value does not depend on earthly success. Thank you that nothing in this life can shake your love for me or change my status as your precious child. Amen.

TEEL WOOL AND TURPENTINE

"In your anger do not sin": Do not let the sun go down while you are still angry.

—Ephesians 4:26

As God's chosen people . . . forgive whatever grievances you may have against one another. Forgive as the Lord forgave you.
—Colossians 3:12–13

The back door slammed. "Mommy, Mommy, I fell down!" Christiana limped into the kitchen and pointed to her bloody big toe.

I scooped her up in my arms and carried her to the couch. She clung to my neck, burying her face in my chest and whimpering. I sat her down and lifted her foot onto my lap.

"No! Don't touch it!" She grabbed my arm and pulled it away from her foot as her energies shifted from the search for comfort to the survival of the fittest.

I brushed her black bangs from her eyes and stroked her cheek. "I need to look at it, Christiana."

The big toe was covered in alternate patches of blood and dirt. I couldn't see the wound. She jerked her foot off my lap. "Don't wash it! It'll hurt!"

"I need to wash it or it will get infected." I used my cheerful it's-going-to-be-all-right voice. Christiana evidently translated my tone as "Mom's sounding too cheerful. It must be really bad." She pulled her knee up to her chest and leaned over to survey the damage. Then she broke into a fresh round of sobs. I tried to pick her up to head to the bathroom, but this time she wasn't clinging to my neck.

"No, no, no!"

I resorted to my firm, authoritative voice. "Come on, Christiana. It won't take long, and then you can go play." She stiffened her body, but I managed to get her onto the bathroom counter. "That's good. You're doing great." I ran a sink of warm water with one hand and held her on the counter with the other. I grabbed a rag and the mild soap and gripped her leg.

Christiana screamed, "No!"

"Christiana, please hold still. It will be done sooner, and it won't hurt so bad."

She splashed and sobbed. "No! Don't. Don't!"

"I've got to get it clean, Christiana. Now stop this."

Christiana lessened the fury of her kicking but still screamed and wiggled as if I were scrubbing with steel wool and turpentine instead of a soft rag and soap. I could see dirt under the loosened skin. The squirming toe, still sporting a faint arc of brown dirt, finally wore me out. I put a bandage on the cut and dried Christiana's tears. She was outside playing in a few minutes.

The next day, I noticed her limping. "Christiana, let me see your toe."

She grabbed my arms when I was several inches away. "Don't touch it."

"I just want to look this time."

Sure enough, her toe showed the red, swollen signs of infection. I sighed and shook my head. Now I would have to enlist Don's help so I could wash the infected wound thoroughly.

Reflections

In the course of living, we all receive emotional and spiritual wounds that need the Father's cleansing touch. Unforgiven hurts may hide under the dirt of denial, pride, fear, or bitterness. When we hold on to grievances against others, we do not hurt them as much as we cripple ourselves. Some deep wounds are too devastating to face alone. The first step in healing may be to seek the help of a pastor or Christian counselor.

Prayer

Dear God, when I am hurt emotionally and the germs of anger and resentment infect my heart, help me to deal with the wounds before I am crippled in my relationships with you and others. Give me humility when my pride keeps me from the cleansing experience of confession, which must precede the healing balm of forgiveness. Give me courage when I fear the cleansing experience of confrontation, which often leads to the restorative ointment of reconciliation. Help me to trust your love to soothe the wounds of my heart. Amen.

TAY CLOSE

Because of the LORD's great love we are not consumed,
    for his compassions never fail.
They are new every morning;
    great is your faithfulness.

— Lamentations 3:22–23

Come near to God and he will come near to you.

— James 4:8

I knelt down and turned Christiana toward me until we established eye contact. "Stay close, Christiana."

She nodded, but her wide eyes darted to a display of coloring books and crayons. To my tactile learner, the touch temptations of a toy store eclipsed all other input.

I had always thought a child harness or wrist leash was an embarrassing reflection of inept, lazy parents. Today I wondered if the toy store carried such a device. I had gained appreciation for these clever parenting tools since Hannah had been born and taken the safe seat in the shopping cart, freeing Christiana to roam. I noted the naive arrogance of my pre-Christiana parenting.

Christiana stood in front of the coloring book display, running her hands over the varied textures of the bright array.

"Come on, Christiana, we need to get a birthday present

for cousin Adrian." I tugged on one of Christiana's hands and pushed the cart with the other. Hannah swung her feet and chewed on the teething ring I had clipped to her shirt.

On our way to the baby doll section, I had to stop every few feet to encourage Christiana to come with us. Christiana paused in front of the rows of green and black plastic and cardboard beckoning from the action figure aisle. Then her mouth dropped open and her eyes widened as we turned the corner into the neon pinks of Barbie land. I took her hand and maneuvered the cart past the smiling faces of the overly mature fashion icons. The pastels of the baby doll area at the end of the aisle paled in comparison to the sea of saturated Barbie hues.

"Christiana, do you want to help me pick out a doll for Adrian?"

"Yes, Mommy."

"Do you see one you like? How about this one? She looks soft and cuddly."

"No."

"You didn't even look at it."

Christiana had never taken much notice of the baby doll we had gotten her for Christmas several months ago. Beyond repeatedly pulling off all the doll's clothes, the cloth and plastic form held little interest.

"How about this one? Look, her eyes close when you lay her down, just like your dolly."

I looked up from the sweet rubber face to find Christiana headed back toward the Barbie end of the aisle. "Don't you want to help?"

She didn't answer.

"Stay in the Barbie section."

No "Yes." No nod. Not even a glance. She stood in front of the bright pink boxes, running her fingers over the cellophane fronts. At least she seldom pulled things off the shelves as she used to. It wouldn't hurt for her to stay there where I could see her while I finished picking out a doll for Adrian.

"What do you think, Hannah?" I held the doll up. Hannah reached for it.

"I don't know. It might be better to find an all-cloth doll. Then Adrian could sleep with her."

I pushed the cart farther down the aisle, examining the vast array of babies that performed every function from acrobatics to potty aerobics. I just wanted a simple rag doll. Didn't they make them anymore? A large cloth doll with a printed face, braided yarn hair, and stitched-on clothes hung from the end of the aisle. Terrific. I pulled her off the hook. Hannah reached for her. Good.

Triumphant in my quest, I sat her in the cart. Now to collect Christiana and get on with the day. I maneuvered my cart around just in time to see Christiana's back disappearing around the opposite end of the aisle. I didn't want to yell across the store, so I spun the cart and pushed around the end in the same direction Christiana had gone. I would intercept her by the action figures. I spied her at the far end of the corridor, absorbed in picking up plastic dinosaurs.

I stopped. Perhaps I should let her get lost for a short while. Maybe experiencing the natural consequence of the fear of being lost would cure her of running off. I backed my way out of the aisle and peered around the corner. Christiana moved a little way down the walkway. She kept up a lively, self-focused conversation and ran her fingers over the boxes as though the packaging were the toy instead of the form inside.

I waited. Two minutes. She hadn't noticed that I wasn't around. Then she looked up and trotted down the aisle toward me.

I smiled and ducked aside, sure she was searching for me. I felt a tickle of guilt at tricking her this way, but she had to learn.

I waited. No Christiana with sad frightened eyes appeared.

I waited. Still, no Christiana.

I peeked around the end. If she had been coming for me, she'd forgotten. She was examining the jump ropes, still cheering herself along with chatter. She headed in the opposite direction.

I couldn't believe it. Was she ever going to notice I was gone? Five minutes of daughter watching had elapsed.

I pushed Hannah and the rag doll to the building-blocks-of-all-sizes section. Christiana stood in front of a bag of large-size blocks in primary colors. The red rope tie at the top was in her hand. I almost intervened, but she let go on her own accord and moved on.

I watched. Six minutes. Eight minutes. Ten minutes, and she still had not noticed my absence.

A man and his son came down the aisle from the opposite side. Christiana stood unaware as they walked by, staring at my unsupervised youngster. Their gaze reminded me that not all people share my values.

I shivered. It was time for my "lost" experiment to end. I passed behind the man and boy and caught up with my precious Christiana.

"Hello, Christiana. Are you having a good time?"

She looked up at me and smiled. "Yes."

"It's time to go."

$\mathcal{R}eflections$

Even when we get so busy that we take off without God, God watches over us, concerned for our safety, waiting for us to turn around and seek the face of the One who loves us most. Whether we've been close all along or have been wandering on our own, it always brings joy to God's heart when we seek his face, acknowledge his loving smile, and take hold of his hand to lead us safely through the day.

Prayer

Dear God, you are my loving parent who never lets me out of sight. Sometimes I let the attractive things of this world distract me from your purposes for me and lure me away from the safety of your loving presence. You do not abandon me when I foolishly wander away. When I look back on my life, I realize that there have been many times when you have protected me from devastating dangers of which I was not aware. You are faithful to me, your child, even when I am not. Thank you. Amen.

Day 14

HE WIND BENEATH MY KITE

"Apart from me you can do nothing. . . . If you remain in me and my words remain in you, ask whatever you wish, and it will be given you. This is to my Father's glory, that you bear much fruit, showing yourselves to be my disciples."

—John 15:5, 7–8

Jesus said, "Peace be with you! As the Father has sent me, I am sending you." And with that he breathed on them and said, "Receive the Holy Spirit."

—John 20:21–22

"You will receive power when the Holy Spirit comes on you."

—Acts 1:8

"Can we bring the kites?" Nathaniel asked. He shifted his weight back and forth in an anticipatory dance.

I glanced out the window at the statue-still trees and took inventory of the amount of stuff we were taking to the park as compared to the number of hands available for carrying. The judgment weighed against it.

"I don't know if that's a good idea. There's not much wind today. We're already taking the Frisbee and the baseball gloves and ball. I have to carry Hannah and the diaper bag. You'll want to spend some time playing on the playground, won't you?"

Nathaniel nodded but twisted one side of his mouth down into a disappointed grimace. His dance ended in a standstill.

"I have to look after Hannah and Christiana, so I won't be able to help you fly the kites. I really think there won't be enough wind but—well, go ask Papa. If it's all right with him, you may bring them."

His head jerked up, and he smiled. "Thanks, Mama," he called on the way down the hall.

Don, Nathaniel, and the play equipment for the day were halfway to the playground before I finished maneuvering Christiana and Hannah out of their car seats.

As Nathaniel walked, the bag holding the kites banged against his legs. The pointed ends of the diamond frames poked through the sides of the thin plastic bag and scraped the ground every few steps.

By the time Hannah toddled to the playground, Nathaniel and Don were kneeling next to the field, untangling our collection of three-dollar flyers from the jumble of loose string and rag-strip kite tails.

"How long has it been since you used these kites?" Don asked.

"Last summer sometime. Try the one with the horse on it. It flies the best. I want the *Sesame Street* one," Nathaniel said.

He reached for a yellow triangle-shaped kite. The faithful toy sported multiple pieces of masking tape bandages attesting to Nathaniel's robust kite-flying adventures of the previous summer.

"You can try," I said, "but you've got to have wind to fly any kite, Nathaniel."

"I can make it fly."

"Let him try it," said Don. He gave me a leave-the-boy-alone look.

"All right. Good luck."

I turned from the kite-flyers and helped Christiana into a swing. Then I picked Hannah up and balanced her on one hip. My strategy was to push the four-year-old with one hand while protecting the two-year-old from harmful encounters with her quick-moving sister. For several concentrated minutes, I accomplished my dual goals.

"Down!" Hannah wiggled and whined, letting me know that watching her sister swing was not her idea of fun.

"Just a minute." I grabbed hold of one of the chains and slowed Christiana to a stop. "Let's go slide now."

I put Hannah down and lifted Christiana out of the swing. They both ran toward the wood-beam fort that housed the slide.

"Look! Hey, Mom, look!" Nathaniel's shout drew my gaze to the field.

Nathaniel was running, his stocky legs churning their maximum speed. Big Bird and Grover rode on the yellow kite, dancing a serpentine path above him at the end of a dozen feet of taut string.

"That's great!" I called as he charged past.

I watched him circle the field with the kite in tow. As he approached the place where Don had started him out, his gait slowed, and the kite looped and crashed into the ground. Nathaniel dragged the kite for several feet through the grass in a hang and jerk pattern, until Don waved him down.

Nathaniel stopped and looked behind him. His shoulders sagged as he walked back to the kite. After a short examination for damages, Don lifted the kite above his head, and Nathaniel trotted forward into launch position.

That boy was determined.

I lifted Hannah onto the short slide, while Christiana attempted to climb up the adjacent wide-beam stairs. A triumphant call from the field drew my attention.

"Mom, look!"

I peered around the edge of the fort. Nathaniel ran by again with his companion kite dancing a few feet behind. I smiled and waved.

"Try letting out some string!" Don yelled from the other end of the field.

Nathaniel glanced down at the roll of string in his hand, his gait slowed and the kite wavered.

I cupped my hand to my mouth. "Don't slow down! Watch out!"

Nathaniel turned toward me. The slight shift in direction sent the kite heading into the ground with the speed of an Olympic diver. The apex of the kite stuck in the ground, and Nathaniel's momentum ripped the plastic front piece from the triangular wings.

This time, no one had to tell him to stop.

Reflections

Sometimes we are called to do work for God's kingdom that is difficult and tiring, but even in those ministries, we need to be sure that we are running on God's strength and direction and not taking off on our own. Remember, not every need we encounter constitutes a call from God for us to act.

Prayer

Dear God, your Holy Spirit is like the wind beneath a kite. Without the empowerment of your Spirit, no matter how well intended, my plans will fail as soon as I stop running with them. When I find myself struggling and exhausted, help me to reexamine whether or not your wind is blowing where I am running. Help me to sense when and where your Spirit is moving. Help me to wait on your guidance and to follow your leading to where you have gone ahead of me, already at work in the hearts of people. Thank you for being the wind beneath the kite of my soul and for upholding me with your loving Spirit. Amen.

EEP DANCING

> *Whatever you do, work at it with all your heart, as working
> for the Lord, not for men, since you know that you will receive
> an inheritance from the Lord as a reward. It is the Lord Christ
> you are serving.*
>
> —Colossians 3:23–24

Christiana bounced on her seat. Her legs swung in anticipatory rhythm as we pulled up to Studio D. My six-year-old was living one of her dreams; she was taking a beginner's dance class with an introduction to gymnastics, jazz, and cheerleading.

Christiana was out of the car, pulling at the handle of the heavy front door almost before I turned the engine off and gathered Hannah from her car seat. I grabbed Christiana's pink dance slippers off the dashboard, and we headed into the excited bedlam of the entryway. Pink and purple coats, piled on top of an assortment of street shoes, backpacks, and dance bags, lined the walls.

Warm-up music pressed the "speed up" button on the several latecomers who were yanking off street shoes and donning dance slippers. Christiana plopped down in the middle of the hall and pulled at her tennis shoes. As she trotted onto the hardwood dance floor, I gathered her things and stuffed them into her bag.

I noticed one of the mothers watching me. I smiled. "One of these days we'll get her here on time."

The woman returned a polite smile and nodded. Next to her lay a neatly folded jacket and a matching lacy pink dance bag with the image of a sparkling ballerina.

All of the seats in the waiting area were filled with parents, so I leaned against the doorway to the studio where I could watch the class. Hannah set down her coloring books and sat at my feet. I wasn't sure why I had her bring things to do; she always watched the lesson.

The studio was bright; the fluorescent lights reflected from the polished floor and wall of mirrors. The warm-up routine was one they had been doing all season, gradually adding to a repetition of simple steps designed to stretch all of the main muscle groups. Although the music had a rapid jazz rhythm, most of the girls followed the "cross-over," "toe-heel," and "kick" commands with ease.

I noticed one little girl wearing a pink leotard with lacy trim and ballerina image that matched the dance bag next to the mother. The girl stood in front of the teacher modeling a mirror image of every twist and turn.

The mother noticed me comparing the image on the dance bag.

"Your daughter dances very well," I said.

"She's been in lessons since she was four."

"That's great."

I sighted Christiana in her place at the end of the back row. She had a half smile on her face, and her eyes were wide. Although she had improved quite a bit and had learned most of the steps, she was consistently two beats behind the group. Her movements were stilted, and she held her hands in front of her in an awkward stance, as if she didn't know quite what to do with them.

She had always been a little different, behind in some ways, but we affirmed her in her uniqueness. I knew that not being the best at something was all right, but she was *so* awkward.

The group repeated the beginning steps of the routine, a simple side-step, side-step that they had been doing for months now. Christiana stepped one way just fine, but she bumped into the little girl next to her as she stepped right again instead of left. She looked at the little girl in a startled awareness of the other's presence.

The teacher walked over and smiled at the bumped girl, sending her back to continue the routine. She moved Christiana a couple of feet further away from the line and then stood beside her showing her for the hundredth time how to reverse directions each step.

The rest of the lesson went downhill. The warm-up was her best routine; the others were more complicated, and they hadn't been working on them as long. Near the end of the lesson, Christiana simply stopped dancing and stood swaying, signaling that her senses were overloaded.

I found myself not wanting to look into the waiting room, not wanting to make eye contact with the mother of the lead dancer. An unwelcome feeling of embarrassment for Christiana snaked its clammy fingers around my throat.

Hannah pulled at my top. I looked down, glad for the distraction.

"She's not very good, is she?" Hannah asked.

I felt my face flush. "She's just fine for Christiana. She does the best she can, and that's all right. People have different strengths and weaknesses, Hannah, but if she wants to take lessons, she may." My voice held an edge of defensive indignation that I hadn't intended.

On the way home, I wondered if taking Christiana to dance was a good thing. I wanted to approach the subject carefully so as not to further embarrass her. I asked, "Christiana, how was your lesson?"

The outburst of her smile squeezed her cheeks up, shaping

her eyes into sparkling crescents. "Great Mommy! I'm getting real good."

Reflections

Most of us can remember a time when we felt awkward and embarrassed because of the response of others to us or because we felt like something we did was not up to standard. God is our perfect heavenly parent who stands near us in those times, smiling with sincere appreciation and clapping for us, for our willingness, for our efforts, for our joy in giving.

Prayer

Dear God, thank you for the voice of your Holy Spirit that guides and comforts and fills me with joy like music fills a dancer. Many days I feel like such an awkward dancer. I look around and observe the wonderful things others are doing for your kingdom. I see their graceful steps of loving hospitality, timely encouragement, or faithful service, and I feel like I have fallen behind the beat and have let you down with my less than perfect performance. Help me to stop comparing myself to others. Help me to remember that you delight in my eager participation more than my accomplishment. Please free me from self-consciousness so that I may live out the joy of dancing to the accompaniment of your loving will for me. Amen.

Day 16

KNOWING IT ALL

Do not deceive yourselves. If any one of you thinks he is wise by the standards of this age, he should become a "fool" so that he may become wise. For the wisdom of this world is foolishness in God's sight.

—1 Corinthians 3:18–19

Do not be wise in your own eyes;
fear the LORD and shun evil.
This will bring health to your body
and nourishment to your bones.
—Proverbs 3:7–8

Four-year-olds are the most remarkable people. Sometime during their fourth year of life they learn everything there is to know. Hannah, my youngest, was particularly adept at this miraculous transformation. One evening, when she was almost five, she announced at the dinner table that she knew everything.

Our eldest, Nathaniel, took this proclamation as a challenge and focused his logical ten-year-old energies on proving her wrong.

"If you know everything, then what is one hundred plus two hundred?" he asked.

Hannah pushed her red curls back from her forehead with an elegant flair. "I know that. . . . I just don't want to tell you."

"You do *not* know."

"Uh-huh, I do."

Nathaniel finished his bite of broccoli and aimed again at Hannah's defenses. "Okay. What's the capital of the United States?"

Hannah's lips puckered and her eyes narrowed. "I know that."

"Then what?"

"I just don't want to tell you."

"You do not."

"I do too." Hannah tilted her head and raised her nose with the airs of a queen facing the inquisitors of an unjust insurrection.

"All right kids, please don't fight," I said.

"But she doesn't know everything," Nathaniel said.

"I do too."

I took an extended wipe at my mouth with a napkin to hide my smile. Don didn't bother to hide his chuckle at her absurd claim of omniscience.

Nathaniel warmed to his task, and the two entertained us with this question and answer game on and off all through supper.

The next morning, we started our routine of breakfast and clean up. Then we were ready for school. At the time, I was homeschooling Nathaniel and Christiana. Hannah wasn't yet the normal age for beginning kindergarten, so I was only teaching her on days when she requested—most days she requested.

Nathaniel took his assignments to the kitchen table and started his work while I gathered Christiana's books and organized myself in the living room. Hannah strolled into the living room and sat down beside me on the couch. I gave her a hug and returned to my lesson plans.

"Can I do reading today, Mommy?" she asked.

"Certainly—"

Like a lion pouncing on its prey, Nathaniel bounded into

the room and pointed an accusing finger at Hannah. "You don't know how to read. You don't know everything!"

Hannah crossed her arms over her chest and flung herself back against the couch cushions. She pulled her knees up in frustration.

"If you know how to read, then Mama doesn't need to teach you," Nathaniel said.

Hannah sat pouting for several seconds, her eyes rapidly shifting as her mind searched for an escape from admitting defeat. Then she scooted herself forward and brushed back her curls.

"So?" she said, recovering her royal demeanor. "I know everything else."

Reflections

Most of us have some area of life where we resist the vulnerability and change that comes with being teachable. We will never understand everything about our lives, including our Christian faith, parenting, or marriage. If asked, we would all agree that God is the only omniscient being, yet, sometimes, we forget that to understand everything is to be God.

Prayer

Dear God, help me to be teachable. Reveal areas where pride in my limited knowledge interferes with your efforts to expand my understanding. Help me to realize that my value is not based on what I know, but on whom you have made me. Heal me of the fear of vulnerability. Help me to have faith in your all-knowing power, so that I may rest in your guidance and be free of the trap of acting like I know it all. Open my heart and mind to the depth of your truth, the breadth of your wisdom, and the wonder of your richness in all of creation. Amen.

SINGING ALONG

The LORD is my strength and my song;
he has become my salvation.
Shouts of joy and victory
resound in the tents of the righteous.
—Psalm 118:14–15

"How does God talk to us if we can't see him?"

Hannah had developed a strategic practice of delaying bedtime for several minutes by asking her tough questions right before I intended to walk out of the room.

I sat back down on the bed. She and I both knew that if I waited until tomorrow to answer her, I would forget. The question was a good one for a five-year-old and worthy of whatever answer I could give.

"God talks to us in many ways—"

"Like what?"

"Are you going to interrupt?"

"Sorry."

"Believe me, I'll try to be as quick as I can. God doesn't talk to me like we talk out loud, but I believe God does communicate with me. Sometimes I know what God is saying through the Bible, which I believe is God's Word. Sometimes I pray about something and then a helpful thought comes into my mind that I believe God puts there in answer to my prayer.

Other times I may have a feeling about something or someone that I know is destructive. I pray to God for help, and my feelings change. I believe that is God talking also."

Hannah shifted her position from leaning on one elbow to laying flat on her pillow. I took the move as a sign.

"Sometimes God talks to me through the words of a writer who was inspired by God to write a book, or sometimes God talks to me through the preacher's sermon or a talk with a friend."

Hannah raised her eyebrows and looked from side to side as if processing with some degree of doubt.

"It's hard to explain. Not everything the preacher says is God talking to me, but sometimes I have a feeling inside that God's Holy Spirit is saying"—I dropped my pitch an octave—"'Listen to this. This is God talking.'"

Hannah smiled and shook her head. "Oh, Mommy."

"You need to get to sleep." I tucked the covers around her shoulders. "You'll know when God talks to you if you're listening."

Hannah looked up at me as though she were a skeptical professor peering over her reading glasses at the outlandish babbling of an imaginative student. She pulled her arms from under the tucked covers and placed them over her stomach. Apparently none of my proposed venues of God's revelation struck a note of reality for her.

The next day, Hannah and I sat in our idling van waiting to pick up Don from a late meeting at work.

Hannah tapped her feet on the floor and stared at her wiggling fingers in her lap as if contemplating the mysteries of the movement of the opposable thumb.

"You know, Mommy, when I'm playing outside and singing songs, if it's a song I know from a movie, I can hear the person from the show singing it, and I try to sing like them. But when I'm singing my own made up songs, it's like I hear the music playing in my head, and I just sing along."

"Wow. That's really neat, Hannah." I prayed a silent "thank you" to God for this teaching opportunity. "Hannah, you know when you asked me about how God talks to you?"

"You mean like last night?"

"Yes. I take it that most of what I said didn't make much sense to you."

She shook her head.

"Perhaps, Hannah, when you hear your music, that is God's special way of talking to you, and when you sing along, it's like you're talking back, saying 'thank you' for the song."

Reflections

God talks to each of us differently, being sensitive to each personality, communication pattern, and life experience. God wants us to experience the joy, excitement, and sense of fulfilled thanksgiving that come when we hear and respond to his voice.

Prayer

Dear God, help me not to limit your communication to certain means and familiar ways. Help me to recognize your voice, your presence, and your plan in every activity of my day by singing along with the music you are eternally playing. Amen.

BABY TEETH

> "Forget the former things;
> do not dwell on the past.
> See, I am doing a new thing!
> Now it springs up; do you not perceive it?"
> —Isaiah 43:18–19

> *Therefore, if anyone is in Christ, he is a new creation; the old has gone, the new has come!*
> —2 Corinthians 5:17

Hannah wiggled her chair away from the table and said, "I'm not hungry."

In the five short years of her life, Hannah had consumed almost as much spaghetti as I had in a lifetime. A refusal to eat spaghetti signaled something more than a full stomach.

"Did you eat too much snack this afternoon?" I asked.

"I didn't have a snack." Hannah's eyes reddened. She turned sideways in her chair and stared at the floor.

Nathaniel piled his plate with noodles. "I bet she ate a bunch of graham crackers. I found the box open on the counter."

"Did not," Hannah scowled at her older brother.

Christiana smiled, "I did."

I shook my head and passed the sauce to Don. "All right, you guys. I know about Christiana eating crackers. I gave her permission." I turned back to Hannah. "What's wrong, Hannah? Are you sick?"

Hannah shook her head and kicked at a dog toy lying under the table.

"Then what's the problem?"

"My tooth hurts."

"Did you hit it on something?" Don asked.

Her shoulders rose and dropped.

Nathaniel rolled his eyes and said, "You don't know if you hit your tooth on something?"

Hannah sniffed.

I gave Nathaniel the lay-off-your-sister-or-else glare and asked Hannah, "Will you let me take a look?"

She nodded.

I knelt in front of her. She raised her head, opened her mouth, and pointed to her top, right incisor. "Ich iz 'is 'un."

I moved the tooth back and forth with unanchored ease. Hannah jerked away.

"Ow!" Her hand clapped over her mouth, and her eyebrows furrowed in betrayed wrath.

"Hannah, it looks like you're getting ready to lose your first baby tooth."

Hannah's eyebrows did a roundabout and raised in question.

"Everyone starts to lose baby teeth at about your age."

"Don't worry. You'll get another one," Nathaniel said.

I sat back down at the table. "Now, how about some dinner. It won't hurt your tooth. Just chew to the side."

Hannah didn't move toward her plate.

"Really. Spaghetti is very soft. You can chew in the back of your mouth. It won't hurt."

Hannah's eyes were wide, and her hand still guarded her mouth. "I don't want a new tooth."

"Hmm. I don't think it's a choice, Honey."

"It's just a matter of time," Don added.

I reached across the table and picked up Hannah's plate to

serve her some supper. "I know you must be hungry. Please try to eat something."

I had learned a number of years prior that you cannot *make* a child eat, so I left her alone and focused conversation on other events of the day. After a few minutes, I noticed her nibbling at her noodles.

I calculated by the easy movement of the tooth that it would be out by the next morning, but Hannah nursed the hanging incisor for two more days, eating little and complaining much. She wanted me to fix it for her, but any mention of pulling the tooth sent her into tears.

I remembered my father with string or pliers in hand. I shuddered, and my stomach knotted up at the memory. Nature would take its course. I would wait her out.

The morning of the third day, Hannah ran from her room grinning. "Look, Mommy!"

I met her halfway down the hall. In the palm of her hand lay the troublesome ivory bit that had come out during the night.

"Terrific!" I herded her into the bathroom and lifted her onto the counter. "Look in the mirror."

Hannah opened her mouth wide and turned her head back and forth, examining the gap. Then she hopped off the counter and wrapped her arms around my waist.

I brushed her bangs back with my fingers. "Was that so bad?"

"Nope. Next time I want you to pull it the very first day."

Reflections

Salvation in Christ makes us a "new creation" not only in the moment of our belief but also throughout our lives. God continues to remake us into the image of Christ, into the fullness of God's unique creation as old things pass away and the new comes.

Prayer

Dear God, at times as I grow spiritually, you make me aware of parts of my personality or habitual ways of perceiving and relating to others that need to change. Just like my children, I get frightened of the unknown and I want to cling to the comfortable ways I've always known. Give me courage to let go when deeper understanding and new behaviors begin pushing out disintegrating ideas and habits. Knowing that my growing is in you, grant me peace. Amen.

Day 19

"CAN I GO NOW?"

"The Counselor, the Holy Spirit, whom the Father will send in my name, will teach you all things and will remind you of everything I have said to you."

—John 14:26

*"As the heavens are higher than the earth,
so are my ways higher than your ways
and my thoughts than your thoughts."*

—Isaiah 55:9

"Mom, I don't get it. Why do we send out so many missionaries? We had so many missionary names in our Sunday school class that we didn't even get through them all."

Hannah had me all to herself for a few minutes while we drove home from dropping Don off at work.

"Hannah, I know it seems like a lot, but there are many people who haven't heard about Jesus."

"But why would someone from another country believe someone they didn't know if they just told them about Jesus?"

"That's a good question. The Bible tells us that we're responsible to tell people about Jesus, and then the Holy Spirit will witness in that person's heart that what we have said is the truth. Then it's up to that person to choose whether or not to believe. Also, the missionaries try to love the people they tell about Jesus. Through their love, they earn the trust of the people."

"But why would someone from another country want to believe?"

"Because knowing Jesus can make a big difference, a positive difference in their lives. Do you remember when Papa went to Africa to videotape the Maasai people and the missionaries working with them?"

Hannah nodded.

"Some of the men in the Maasai tribe had been very angry. They resented the white people coming to their land with different American ways. They sometimes spent their money on drinking alcohol, a problem also introduced by the white people. Then when they were drunk, they were mean to their families. . . ."

I noticed Hannah was now looking out of the window instead of at me. *Time to wrap it up.*

"When they came to know Jesus, they stopped drinking, and the Holy Spirit helped them to forgive and not be so angry anymore. No matter what the customs, Jesus is for—"

"Mom, I don't get it—how Jesus and God can both be God at the same time. I mean if Jesus is God's Son, how can they be the same?"

"Hannah, that's a good question, but please don't interrupt."

I thought for a moment.

"First of all, we probably will never totally understand how that works until we get to heaven. But there are a couple of ways that are helpful to me in understanding that mystery. One way is to think about water. You know water can be ice or liquid, like how we drink it, or steam."

"What does that have to do with God?"

"Just listen for a moment. Are steam and liquid water and ice all the same thing? Are they all water?"

Hannah nodded.

"It's sort of like Jesus is like the solid ice, when he came to

Earth where we could see him; God in heaven is like the liquid water; and the Holy Spirit is like steam, the presence of God in our lives that is real but we cannot see."

"Oh."

Hannah's "Oh" held a bigger message: "Whatever you say, Mom. I still don't get it, but I don't want you to go on talking about it."

"Probably you need to be a little older."

We pulled into the driveway.

"But if I don't understand, how can I tell other people about Jesus? And what if they get mad at me or something."

"Hannah, I think of it sort of like selling Girl Scout cookies."

Hannah wrinkled her forehead again, pulled in her chin, and tilted her head in her "You've got to be kidding" pose. She pulled the handle on the van door and pushed it open with her foot.

"Just hear me out. You know I hate to sell stuff to other people. We don't even sell the candy bars from school; we just donate. But I don't feel bad at all about selling Girl Scout cookies because I know that people *want* to buy them. Some people look forward to cookie sale time every year, and they thank you for selling cookies to them. Right?"

"Yeah."

"I believe that every person deep inside *wants* to know Jesus. Every person wants to be happy and loved. Right?"

Hannah nodded, but her eyes were on the front door to the house, not on me.

"I believe that knowing Jesus is the only way they'll ever—"

"Can I go now?"

"I'd like you not to interrupt me, Hannah."

"Sorry."

"But, yes, you may go."

Hannah jumped out of the van and pushed the door shut. I would have to hold the rest of that thought until another day.

Reflections

When we ask God questions, we need to have patience and trust that God will answer us when the time is right. We'll never have the ability to comprehend some things during this lifetime, and so we must trust God to hold the answers for us. There is a certain peace when we say, "I don't know, but I know the One who does."

Prayer

Dear God, I am a child who asks you many questions. Help me to realize that sometimes I'm not yet ready to hear the answers. Give me the patience to wait on your wisdom and timing and to not walk out on you when your answer is not what I want to hear. Help me to make peace with the fact that the answers to certain questions will always be beyond my understanding. Thank you for your affirming love that enables me to trust you when my questions go unanswered or I don't understand. Amen.

Day 20

Moonwalkers

In God I trust; I will not be afraid.

—Psalm 56:4

*We are hard pressed on every side, but not crushed; perplexed,
but not in despair; persecuted, but not abandoned; struck down,
but not destroyed. . . . [The Lord] said to me, "My grace is
sufficient for you, for my power is made perfect in weakness."*
—2 Corinthians 4:8–9; 12:9

We walked to the lively block party our church was sponsoring for neighborhood outreach.

"Hey, kids, why don't you go and bounce off the walls for a while," Don grinned.

"Right, Papa," Hannah said.

"Papa's not kidding," I said. "Look, it's a moonwalker cage."

I pried my hand loose from Christiana's grip and pointed to the inflated red rubber room bobbling about on the church parking lot next to the dunk tank. Squeals of delight and the rhythmic chanting of the lyrics to the VeggieTales theme came from within. A dozen barefoot and sock-footed children stood in line.

"It sounds fun," said Don.

Nathaniel ripped off his shoes and tossed them into the pile of grungy sneakers belonging to the moonwalker participants.

"Come on, girls, it'll be fun."

"I want to play games first," Christiana said.

"You mean, you're scared to go in there, and you want to win some candy," said Nathaniel.

I raised one eyebrow in reproach. "That's enough, Nathaniel. I'll be glad to go with Christiana to the games."

"I want to go with Mommy," said Hannah, eyeing the swaying, cement-anchored, over-sized balloon room.

The young woman managing the line for the moonwalker cage fiddled with the fastener for the moonwalker entrance.

"Next group!"

Half a dozen children with smiling faces slid off the three-foot cushion of air and plopped down on the sun-baked asphalt to put on their shoes.

I turned to the girls. "Are you sure you don't want to try it? You can both get in on this turn."

In answer, Christiana let go of my hand and headed across the parking lot toward the game area.

Hannah hesitated, then said, "I'll try." She took in a nervous breath and bent over to untie her shoes.

"All right. Have fun!"

As I walked across the lot toward Christiana, I secretly wished the age limit for the bouncing cage was forty instead of ten.

The steady hum of the air pump filling the moonwalker cage vibrated throughout the carnival area. Hannah and Nathaniel jumped their way to breathless bliss several times, becoming enthusiastic promoters who bombarded Christiana with propaganda aimed at getting her into the moonwalker cage. A couple of times Christiana got in line and then decided against the adventure when it came her turn.

Finally, her approach-avoidance bind took a turn to the pro. She discarded her shoes and climbed into the cushioned chamber. Children jumped and bounced from bottoms, to feet, to knees, into the side netting, and onto the center cushion, laughing and talking. Christiana laced her fingers through the netting of one of the sides and held on. She planted her feet wide apart on the undulating billows beneath her. Her whole body tensed against the up and down motion of the shifting cushion.

Nathaniel walked around to the side next to Christiana and said, "Let go. Bounce. It's fun!"

Christiana shifted her gaze to him in recognition and then back to the task of maintaining her vertical orientation.

"Come on, Christiana," Hannah said. "You can't get hurt."

Christiana turned her head in recognition. A boy half her size in weight bounced by like a speeding Energizer bunny. The cushion swelled and sank under Christiana's feet throwing her forward. She released the netting and fell to her hands and knees.

I held my breath.

Christiana turned to her sibling audience; a huge smile and wide eyes commanded her face. "It doesn't hurt!"

Nathaniel rolled his eyes. "Of course it doesn't hurt."

"I can bounce!" Christiana stood up and joined the ruckus, jumping and laughing.

Reflections

Sometimes we hold on to things and relationships in our lives with the fierce grip of the fear of falling or losing control. Our children, our jobs, our spouses, our family of origin, our friends—any of these can be sticking points with us when it comes to trusting God to take care of the people and things in our lives.

Remember: Fear immobilizes us. Faith frees us!

Prayer

Dear God, how I hate to fall! Often I feel insecure, tensing against the ever-changing, undulating currents of my life. Lord, help me to let go of control and to trust in you. Help me to remember that even though I may lose my balance at times and get bumped down, your mercy and grace will never let me fall so hard that I can't get up. Help me to relax my feverish grip so I can bounce along on the gentle rhythms of your love cushion and experience the joy you desire for me during my turn at life. Amen.

Day 21

MEANING TO MEMORIES

And we know that in all things God works for the good of those who love him, who have been called according to his purpose.

—Romans 8:28

Every year, the beginning of summer signaled the annual round of deliberations about what to do with the rubble pile parked in the far corner of our yard. I suggested creating a flower garden amidst the mix of odd-sized rocks, cement-trimmed bricks, and broken Bedford stone. Don preferred hiring someone to haul them away. But every year, more pressing work pushed the rocks from our plans until the grass grew up through the pile, obscuring it from sight and mind.

One summer day, the high-pitched creak of the door leading from our kitchen to the backyard warned me that an interruption to my morning writing session was imminent. I glanced at my watch. The children had been self-contained for over an hour—remarkable. They were old enough to take care of themselves, but at ages six, eight, and eleven, minor squabbles or the slightest injuries constituted a mother-required emergency.

Nathaniel strode into the dining room. His face and clothes

were dirt-streaked; blades of grass poked through the muddy mortar coating his knees. "Mom," he said, "come and see what we made."

"Right now? Or can this wait a while?"

His gazed shifted to the floor, and his smile vanished.

"Just a minute." I pressed the "save" icon and pushed the shortcut series of keys to place my computer in suspension mode.

Nathaniel bounded ahead of me to the tree covered half-lot occupying the far end of our backyard. Christiana and Hannah stood next to a small wall. The barrier stood about two feet high and was around three-and-a-half feet long. The building materials had come from our neglected rubbish quarry.

"The girls brought over the rocks, and I built it."

I examined the results of his engineering feat. He had chosen differing sizes of discards that fit neatly together in a congruous pattern four levels high.

"That's really something. What are you going to use it for?"

"I don't know."

Nathaniel squinted his eyes and wrinkled his forehead. I had asked a practical question about a creative work—my mistake.

"Your granddad, the engineer, would be proud. I'll go get the camera. We'll send him a picture."

A couple of weeks later, the torrential Midwest thunderstorms of early summer flooded one corner of our yard. The water filled a triangular patch spanning adjacent sides of the chain link fence. A ten-by-six-foot hill of dirt rose above the swampy corner pond like a deserted island complete with a singular, lonely tree.

The children made a game of trying to find a way to reach the island without getting wet. They tried floating across on firewood logs and plywood rafts. They tried to pole vault across. Finally, they disassembled Nathaniel's artful wall and stacked the rocks along one side of the fence, and across the stepping stones they went.

As the late-summer heat dried up the pond, the dirt island became the sight of a brush hut. The rocks and stones were recycled again into a floor for the fort then later the foundation of a brush wall.

We mowed the long grass where the rocks had been stacked and heaved a sigh of relief that our landscaping problem was solved. What we considered rubbish turned out to be a treasure trove of creative building supplies.

Reflections

In the back corners of our minds, most of us have discarded piles of broken pieces of our lives—unfulfilled dreams, secret embarrassments, painful disappointments, chipped and battered relationships. The grasses of time and neglect grow up and hide them well so that for periods of time we can pretend they don't exist. But, as the seasons of life change, the grasses die down, and we can't ignore them.

We often don't feel like we have the energy or the resources to deal with the broken pieces of our pasts. But we can lift each of these memories into God's presence and place them in the hands of the Holy Spirit. Then we can listen to God's guidance. Sometimes counseling or sharing with a friend is the venue to which God leads us. We can trust that when we make these things available for God's use, he will bring order and good even to those experiences we consider the most useless or shattered.

Prayer

Dear God, help me to face the rubbish piles of my mind and emotions with your creative, healing Spirit. You are the one who can organize the broken pieces and forgotten memories of my life into creative works. With you as my guide, I can reach into those piles and find treasures and building blocks to strengthen and enrich my life and my service to you. Thank you for using all things for my eternal good. Amen.

OO MANY QUESTIONS

"Ask and it will be given to you; seek and you will find; knock and the door will be opened to you. For everyone who asks receives; he who seeks finds; and to him who knocks, the door will be opened."

—Luke 11:9–10

Let us then approach the throne of grace with confidence, so that we may receive mercy and find grace to help us in our time of need.

—Hebrews 4:16

"Hannah, do you want to watch this video with us?" Don asked our six-year-old music lover, who enjoyed southern gospel.

"Sure." Hannah skipped down the hall and joined me on the couch. Don started the tape and sat on Hannah's other side. A rapid-beat, high-energy melody filled with echoing lines and four-part harmony began the program. Hannah bounced her feet against the couch in rhythm.

Unlike most concert videos, this program showed a room full of artists singing songs together, praying, laughing, and telling stories to each other in casual spontaneity. Watching the program, I felt less like an audience member and more like a neighbor who had dropped in on a family reunion. The people were of all ages, from excited teenagers to silver-haired saints. Their faces and reactions reflected a wide range of emotions and life experiences.

The camera cut to a close-up of a woman worshiping with hands lifted and eyes focused on the unseen heavenly glories as she sang.

"Why does she lift her hands?" asked Hannah.

"Some people like to lift their hands while they worship as a physical sign of lifting God up in glory and opening themselves up to God's blessing."

"Oh."

The camera cut to a shot of two elderly women.

"Why are those people so old?"

I looked over at Hannah in surprise. "What do you mean 'so old'?"

"I mean, most famous singers are younger."

"Well, these women have been singing gospel music all of their lives. They started when they were much younger, and they're on this show sort of like the grandmothers of the group. Everyone respects and loves them because they have been faithful and have sung for and loved God for many years."

"Oh."

The song ended and the leader gave a short welcome speech. The group laughed at a joke and then launched into a song about heaven's happy days.

"Are all those people famous?"

"It depends on what you mean by famous. Some of the people are better known singers than others in the group. People who listen to this kind of music would know who many of them are. But other people who aren't Christians or who don't listen to gospel music wouldn't know who any of them are."

Hannah nodded.

The music transitioned into a worship tune with a slow, lilting rhythm. The camera faded from shot to shot, following the movement of uplifted hands and bowed heads.

"Why does he close his eyes like that when he's singing?"

"This song is sort of like a prayer if you listen to the words. I suppose he wants to think about God and not be distracted by the things around him."

"Oh."

"Why does she touch her nose like that?"

"I think it itches," Don said.

"Oh."

"What are they singing about?"

"They're singing about God making everything in creation," I said, "and how God made us for the purpose of loving us. It says that even before we were made, God knew us and looked into the future and loved us and gave up Jesus to save us."

"Oh."

"Why is that lady crying? Is she sad?"

I sighed. "I don't think she's sad. She probably just feels a lot of strong emotions. Sometimes people cry when they are very happy."

"Oh."

The worship song ended, and one of the leaders handed a microphone to a young man who stood and led a prayer. For a minute we sat on the couch listening. Then a child's curious voice interrupted the prayer.

"Why is his hair long?"

"Hush, Hannah, they're praying," I said.

"Sorry," she whispered.

The prayer over, she repeated the question. "Why is his hair long like a girl's?"

"I don't know." Don's voice had that I-might-know-but-I-don't-want-to-take-the-time-to-say-right-now tone.

I felt the need to address the topic further. "Some men like to wear their hair long. In some places in the world, all of the men, even fierce warriors, wear long hair. It doesn't mean he's like a girl. It doesn't matter so much what people look like on the outside. It's the inside that counts."

"Why do those ladies wipe their eyes like that?"

I gave a do-you-want-to-answer-this-one glance to Don.

When the answer to her question was not forthcoming, Hannah looked up at me and then at her father. "Am I asking too many questions?"

Reflections

How wonderful that we are children of an eternal God, so awe-full and all-powerful, who is yet sitting next to us, available to us when we call to him. We are free to ask God anything. God is bigger than all of our questions.

Prayer

Dear God, I am so glad that you never tire of my questions. Thank you for giving me a mind that seeks to understand. Help me not to seek knowledge for its own sake or to build my pride or feelings of security. Keep me from worshiping knowledge that some day will pass away. Help me to use the understanding I gain from you to serve you and others and to worship you more fully. Amen.

WEED HARVESTING

Praise be to the God and Father of our Lord Jesus Christ, who has blessed us in the heavenly realms with every spiritual blessing in Christ. For he chose us in him before the creation of the world to be holy and blameless in his sight. In love he predestined us to be adopted as his [children] through Jesus Christ, in accordance with his pleasure and will.

—Ephesians 1:3–5

The lawn treatment man comes to my door every summer offering to transform my lawn into a picture perfect landscape of which the neighbors will be envious. Inevitably, my yard has perfect attendance; I mean, every weed on the man's evaluation list is checked as present. I smile and thank him for the free estimate, recommending that he spend his time next year on a more profitable venture. My clover claps its leaves, and the dandelions lift up their yellow faces and smile as the lawn man drives away.

"Mommy, Mommy," Christiana and Hannah yelled as they slammed the back door and ran into the kitchen.

"Yes, what is it?"

"Look what we got you," Christiana said.

Each girl held out a bouquet of hastily picked wildflowers from the yard.

"Thank you." I reached out to receive the gifts from their

sweaty palms. Several of the blossoms fell, blending with the flower pattern on the linoleum.

"They don't have very long stems, do they?" I said.

"I tried to get them long," Hannah said.

"It's all right."

I squatted down and gathered them into a pile. After retrieving the fugitive flowers, I gave each girl a hug, and they darted out the door.

"We'll get you some more," called Christiana over her shoulder.

"That'll be fine."

My answer was lost to the banging of the back door. I found a decorative jelly jar and filled it with water. Then I examined the crushed and bent stems of the flowers I'd laid out on the counter. The purples of the wild violets and the white and delicate pink of the clover nicely complimented the bold yellow of the dandelions. I arranged the bouquet the best I could, floating the shortest-stemmed blossoms near the edges. Then I set the jar on the dinner table.

At supper that evening, Hannah sighed, looking at the flowers. "Do you know what my favorite flower is?" she asked.

"Roses?" Don asked.

She shook her head.

"Tulips?" I guessed.

"No."

"I know. The purple giant columbine out front. I know you like purple," Nathaniel said.

"Nope."

"Dandelions!" Christiana said.

Hannah smiled. "Yep."

"Me too," said Christiana.

"When I was growing up," I said, "I remember Mamaw out in the yard on her hands and knees with the hand spade, digging up dandelions, roots and all, from our lawn. She would have been glad for you to take all of her dandelions away."

"She didn't like them?" Hannah asked.

"No. They're weeds." Nathaniel shook his head.

"But they're pretty," Christiana said.

"What makes something a weed?" asked Hannah.

"A weed is any plant that people don't want to grow in a certain place," Don answered.

"Oh," said Hannah. "Well, I want dandelions in our yard. So, at our house, dandelions aren't weeds."

Reflections

In order to gain acceptance, many Christians find themselves adhering to unspoken rules of appearance and behavior that are more cultural than biblical. Many of us have been in a situation, at church or elsewhere, where we were made to feel like unwanted weeds among a group of flowers.

Jesus showed the socially unacceptable people of his time that they were beautiful and valuable.

Prayer

Dear God, help me to throw off the blinders of society and to see the beauty of your creation with the clear eyes of a child. When I feel rejected and out of place, help me to see myself still as a beautiful flower purposefully planted in your garden. Forgive me for shunning people who society stereotypes as undesirable. Help me always to value others as you do and to receive their presence in my life as a gift. With childlike delight, help me to seek the signs of your budding blossoms in my life and in every person's life. Amen.

$\mathcal{U}$NBEARABLE PUNISHMENT

If we claim to be without sin, we deceive ourselves and the truth is not in us. If we confess our sins, he is faithful and just and will forgive us our sins and purify us from all unrighteousness. . . . And so we know and rely on the love God has for us.

God is love. Whoever lives in love lives in God, and God in him. Love is made complete among us so that we will have confidence on the day of judgment.

—1 John 1:8–9; 4:16–17

Striding through the kitchen on my way to the laundry room, basket in hand, clothes piled to my chin, I spied the corner of a cookie box peeking out from under the table. I backed up for a closer look. I was sure I had put away that box after packing the children's lunches. I set my basket down and picked up the box. No oatmeal cream cookie sandwiches. Someone had helped himself or herself to an unapproved afternoon snack.

I hefted the laundry basket back onto my hip and headed downstairs. The medieval music and pinging alarms of Nathaniel's favorite computer game floated up the stairwell. The ever hungry eleven-year-old might have lapsed in his self-discipline.

"Nathaniel, do you know anything about the oatmeal cream cookies?"

"No. Is it snack time?"

"Not any more. The cookies are gone."

"Oh, man! You might check with Christiana." His voice held the disappointed indignation of an honest answer.

"Thanks."

I loaded dirty clothes into the washer and scooped the clean clothes into the basket from the dryer. I felt a twinge of discomfort about Nathaniel assuming Christiana had eaten the cookies. I didn't want to scapegoat her automatically whenever something went awry in the house. She always claimed she wanted to do what was right whenever we talked about right and wrong, but she seemed to lack the self-control needed to resist temptation. Her mental disabilities came with a heavy dose of impulsiveness.

Should I use more severe consequences? Should I just lock up everything that might tempt her as if she were still a two-year-old? Perhaps another round of rewards for days when she didn't break any house rules would do the trick. My stomach tensed and my lips tightened. I was so tired of dealing with her.

I threw the last sock into the basket and headed back up the stairs. Hannah was on her way down.

"Hannah, do you know anything about the empty cookie box in the kitchen?" My voice reflected my frustration and had an accusatory edge.

"No. I didn't eat any cookies. Ask Christiana."

Sigh.

Christiana had a sweet tooth the size of a mastodon tusk. I dropped the basket of clean clothes on the couch and grabbed the cookie box. Then, I stomped back to Christiana's bedroom where she was playing with her papers from school.

I watched at the doorway for a minute. I spied a smear of white on the corner of Christiana's mouth that looked suspiciously like the filling from an oatmeal cream cookie sandwich.

What am I going to do with her?

The tension in my stomach crawled up into my throat. I

swallowed, wanting to be calm and unbiased, as a good parent should be in these situations.

"Christiana, I need to ask you something."

She looked up from her play. I held up the empty cookie box.

"Do you know anything about these cookies?" I spat the words out short and quick. My arms were folded tightly across my chest.

Christiana's chin dropped open, and her eyes darted back and forth. She had read the anger in my voice. "What's the consequence?" she asked.

"Well, I don't know yet. Did you eat these cookies?"

"Tell me the consequence." She stared at me with wide eyes.

"Oh, Christiana, I suppose whoever ate the cookies will not get dessert tonight, in his or her lunch tomorrow, or for supper tomorrow night."

She looked down and fingered the paper in her hands. "No time-out?"

"I guess not."

"No spanking?"

"Of course not."

"Do you still love me?"

My anger drained away. "Yes, of course I still love you."

"I did it."

"Thank you for telling me the truth, Christiana."

"No dessert for two nights?"

"That's right."

She came over and hugged me, looking up into my eyes.

"Christiana, was it worth it to take the cookies? Was that a good decision?"

"Sorry. I won't do it next time."

I wiped the dab of white cream from the corner of her mouth. "I'm sure you won't."

Reflections

The story of the gospel is the story of a heavenly parent who longs to forgive us and restore us to a relationship with himself. Jesus has taken upon himself the unbearable consequence of separation from God through his death on the cross. When we confess our wrong deeds or attitudes, God will forgive us so that we can carry a confident feeling of relief, rest, and peace into our day.

Prayer

Dear God, I often feel like a fearful child when I do things that I know displease you. I doubt your love and hesitate to confess my sins, willing to live with my guilt in order to avoid facing you. Bring to my heart and mind sins that need confessing. Help me to face, with your grace, the natural consequences for the wrong decisions I make. Thank you, Lord, that your arms are always open for a reassuring hug when I come to you and confess. Amen.

PAINT ROLLERS AND MESSY WALLS

There are different kinds of gifts, but the same Spirit. There are different kinds of service, but the same Lord. There are different kinds of working, but the same God works all of them in all [people].

—1 Corinthians 12:4–6

He who began a good work in you will carry it on to completion until the day of Christ Jesus.

—Philippians 1:6

"Can I help?"

I hesitated. The image of my six-year-old with a paint roller in hand conjured up latex nightmares of ruined clothes and two-tone hair—not the natural kind. But the fifteen-foot expanse of scuffed and dirtied living room wall ahead of me said, "Why not? Look at me. She couldn't possibly make me look worse!"

I forced a smile and answered, "Okay, Hannah. Go and put on some old clothes and your hat."

I poured paint into a second paint pan and extended the drop cloth further down the wall. The happy little house painter was back before I finished. I encased her in a smock and twirled her red curls into a knot under her hat.

"Watch how I get the paint on the roller. It needs to be covered evenly. Start by making an 'N' or 'Z' pattern, like this, and then smooth it out with up-and-down strokes, like this."

"Sure, Mom."

"Hey, why does she get to paint?" Christiana interrupted our painting lesson.

"She's getting to paint because she asked."

"Can I paint too?"

Before I could answer, Nathaniel walked in and asked, "Do I get to help, too?"

"If you ask politely."

"Can I *please* paint?"

"Please?" echoed Christiana.

"*May* I please paint, and yes, you may, after you go change into old clothes."

In ten minutes, my line of apprentice painters had been instructed and was in full swing. I had traded in my roller for a foreman's cap and was walking up and down the ranks grimacing and critiquing. I noted a straying drip. "Hannah, look here, you need to—"

As I pointed to a bead of dripping paint, Christiana's roller grazed my arm and the sleeve of my T-shirt. "Oh, Honey," I said. It wasn't that my T-shirt was that valuable, but it was an old favorite.

"Sorry, Mommy." She stared at my sleeve. Paint from her roller streamed onto the drop cloth.

I grabbed the handle and placed the roller back in the pan. "You have got to pay attention if you're going to do this."

"Sorry, Mommy."

This time her apology was accompanied with downcast eyes. When I'm in task mode, being affirming is not one of my strong suits. I lightened my tone and smiled. "It's all right, Sweetie. We can clean this up."

She nodded.

"How about using a brush for a while. Would you trade, Hannah?"

Hannah took an intercepting swipe at the identified drip and replied, "Sure."

Christiana took the more manageable brush with a grateful smile.

"Now, nobody step in this paint puddle while I get a paper towel."

I stood in the doorway on my return and surveyed the work. The wall looked somewhat like a modern art mural. Like the silhouette of the buildings in a city skyline, the height of each paint plot corresponded to the heights of my children. Patches of greenish ivory showed through the tannish mauve in uneven strips and blotches as if they were meant to represent misplaced doors and skewed windows. But at least the paint was getting on the wall.

"You guys are doing great," I encouraged. I kept a watchful eye on Christiana's brush as I stooped to wipe up the paint spill. "Make sure you fill in all the spots."

The painters responded by increasing the fervor of their strokes.

The phone rang. I answered and stood in the doorway talking. My eyes wandered over the busy painters, but my mind was on the conversation. Ten minutes later, I hung up and focused once more on the living room wall. Many of the doors and windows of the city mural had disappeared, and the spaces between the buildings had almost vanished.

Christiana put her brush down and wiped her hand on her smock. "Mommy, I don't want to paint anymore."

"That's fine." I untied her smock and steered her into the kitchen to wash the mauve latex from her fingers.

Hannah joined us at the sink then Nathaniel came in, his trash-bag smock in hand. "Can we stop, too?"

As they finished washing, I felt relieved. "Thanks for helping, kids." I knew my appreciation was more heartfelt in acknowledging their good intention than for the actual help in painting. Many tasks seemed easier to do myself, but I knew the training was valuable for their sakes.

I walked back into the living room and turned on some energizing music. I placed the extra brush and roller in the empty pan to soak in water and started back on the wall. For the next half hour, I played a game of connect-the-paint-plots-and-find-and-obliterate-the-hidden-green-splotches. In spite of the necessary new technique involved in this type of painting, I found that I made progress much more quickly than I had expected. The children really had helped me.

That night at dinner, Hannah and Christiana bragged to Don about their painting accomplishments. Don raised one eyebrow and looked at me with amused sympathy.

I pointed to the wall. "They did help."

Don waited for me to add a "but" at the end of my praise.

"No, really. They did great."

Hannah sat forward and asked, "Does this mean we get to help tomorrow?"

Reflections

Sometimes we find ourselves hesitating to begin work on a ministry to which we feel called because we fear failure, doubting our abilities or dreading the criticism of others. Be assured that God is the master painter and will be faithful to finish whatever we begin in his name.

Prayer

Dear God, you are a heavenly parent who understands that my work in your house isn't perfect. I am so glad that I can count on you to go before me preparing the way and to come behind me filling in the places I miss. You even know that I will, now and then, spill a bit of paint and make a mess or tarnish your garments with a misplaced swipe. How faithful you are to raise me up in my capabilities, and how amazing you are to turn even my faltering efforts into beautiful and effective works in your house. Thank you for your patient guidance. Amen.

IRTY FEET

*[Jesus] got up from the meal, took off his outer clothing, and
wrapped a towel around his waist. After that, he poured water
into a basin and began to wash his disciples' feet, drying them
with the towel that was wrapped around him.*

*He came to Simon Peter, who said to him, "Lord, are you
going to wash my feet?"*

*Jesus replied, "You do not realize now what I am doing,
but later you will understand."*

*"No," said Peter, "you shall never wash my feet." Jesus
answered, "Unless I wash you, you have no part with me."*

—John 13:4–8

W*hy did we come to the Maundy Thursday service?* Of course, I
knew it was one of the most important church events of the
year. It was important for the children to eat a Passover meal
and hear about Christ as the lamb slain for our sins. It was
also important to think about Jesus' teaching on servanthood,
symbolized in the foot washing service.

But it seemed like the children hadn't heard a word of what
the pastors were saying. They preferred chicken to the lamb.
They didn't like the salad and bitter herbs, symbolizing the
slavery of the Israelites in Egypt, or the nuts and apples,
symbolizing the mortar of the Hebrew's slave work. Christiana
spilled her grape juice, and Nathaniel just about choked on a

piece of parsley he popped in his mouth to show off. I sat at the table feeling tired and irritable.

Maybe the foot washing service would go better. Oh, no! I had forgotten all about the foot washing. I blushed as I envisioned my hairy legs and dirty feet. I usually washed my feet and shaved my legs before the foot washing service; it shouldn't matter, but—well, it just did. I had been so busy getting ready to go out of town to visit my in-laws that I hadn't thought everything through. In fact, we had decided to come just at the last minute.

I looked across the table at Hannah. She was systematically destroying her Styrofoam cup by pinching little pieces off the sides and dropping them in the middle.

"Hannah, stop that," I whispered.

She set the cup on the table and gave it a push, upsetting the base and sending a shower of styro-snow onto the floor.

She covered her mouth and raised her eyebrows in an "Oops" expression.

I shook my head. We would clean it up when the service was over.

Christiana leaned over and said, "I've got to go potty."

"Right now? Can't you wait until this is done?"

"I've got to go bad."

"All right. You know where the bathroom is, but please try to be quiet."

The legs of Christiana's chair screeched against the tiled floor. She loped out of the room as I smiled my apologies to the half-dozen onlookers who had turned toward the disturbance. *Oh, why did we come?*

The leader's voice drew our attention to the podium. "For all who wish to stay for foot washing, please bring your chairs and arrange them in circles near the basins and towels during the next hymn."

"Do you kids want to stay?" I asked Nathaniel and Hannah, hoping they would say no.

"I think we should," Don said. "Grab a chair."

This would truly be a lesson in humility. We joined another family forming a circle. Christiana joined us.

"I want to wash Mommy's feet." Nathaniel's declaration surprised me.

"Me too," said Hannah and Christiana together.

"Well, all right." I sat in a chair and pulled off my socks and shoes. Don went with Nathaniel to get a basin and a towel.

Nathaniel knelt down on the floor in front of me and said, "Okay, Mommy."

I felt a strange urge to stop him from washing my feet. It wasn't embarrassment about my leg hairs; his sense of cultural no-nos hadn't developed that far. It just felt wrong for him to be washing me. I had washed him when he was little, and I still washed his scrapes and cuts.

I awkwardly lifted my foot and set it in the basin. He splashed the warm water over my foot, then I lifted it onto the towel he held in his lap.

He smiled.

Whether he was just enjoying playing with the water or whether he understood the meaning of serving another, I couldn't tell, but he was beaming with enjoyment. We repeated the procedure with the other foot. I tried to think of something to say, but all I could get out was, "Thank you."

Then Hannah and Christiana washed my feet. Their little hands stroked my feet so lightly that it tickled. I had to hold the weight of my feet up while they dried them. They returned the basin and towel and then grabbed me from both sides for dual hugs.

"I love you, Mommy," Hannah said.

"Me too," said Christiana.

"I love you, too," I answered.

I started to get up to wash someone else's feet, but the service was coming to a close. I put my socks and shoes back on. I didn't feel tired and irritable anymore. I felt loved and peaceful and, yes, humbled. Not because my feet had been dirty or my legs hairy—the children hadn't noticed. I felt humbled because I had been on the receiving end of my children's love, forced to sit still and accept their service without giving back or rushing off to the next task.

That's why I had come tonight, to have Jesus wash my feet. Christ's love had flowed through the splashing water and the gentle touches of my children.

Reflections

Could it be that, at times, Christ is the one asking to serve us through the service of others? Why do we often find it difficult to let others serve us? One reason may be that we stay in control by being the one in charge. When we ask others to help us, we may feel vulnerable or indebted to them.

Prayer

Dear God, I am entrenched in the habit of serving. Help me to receive your ministry to me through your Spirit and through the people in my life. Help me to allow myself to be vulnerable enough to receive from others with humble gratitude, especially my children's love when they offer it to me. Open my eyes to opportunities to affirm the value of their gifts by looking in their eyes and holding each hug and smile as a sacred offering. Amen.

ISABLED DREAMS

*"All your [children] will be taught by the LORD, and great will
be your children's peace."*

—Isaiah 54:13

*"For I know the plans I have for you," declares the LORD, "plans
to prosper you and not to harm you, plans to give you hope
and a future."*

—Jeremiah 29:11

"So, what can we expect for Christiana's future?" Don's words
were casual, but his voice held an underlying tension.

The social worker at the children's hospital hesitated, then
said, "Well, she can certainly train for a vocational job in high
school and most likely be competitive in a vocational setting.
She possibly could live independently or in a group home setting, and she even might be able to marry. You just never know."
She spoke as if she were telling us good news about our seven-
year-old mildly autistic and mentally handicapped daughter.

Don and I sat in silence. It had been a long day of IQ testing, language and speech testing, sensory integration dysfunc-
tion testing, and interviews for Don and me. I had come to
the hospital hoping to gain some further understanding of
our middle child that would help me parent her better. She
was "a study" as my Grandma Stannie would say.

I had never thought about her long-term future. Although the room was plenty warm, I shivered. *Might be able to marry? Possibly live independently?* These were things I had taken for granted for all my children. Not that they all needed to marry or go to college or leave home the day after their eighteenth birthdays, but, without thinking about it, I had expected that they all could do these things if they chose to do them. I had certain dreams for them. I hoped they would experience the same joy, growth, and sense of accomplishment I had experienced in life.

Christiana bounded into the room ahead of the speech pathologist who had been entertaining her during our debriefing. Christiana threw herself onto the couch next to me and hugged me. She had enjoyed all of the attention. It wasn't often that she got to be with both Don and me without her brother and sister.

I smiled down into her face, radiant with affection. I fought back the tears threatening to fill my eyes. *She doesn't know what she might miss. Oh, Christiana, my sweet Christiana.* I pushed her page-boy bangs off her forehead and kissed her.

The director stood and offered her hand. "If you have any more questions, don't hesitate to call."

I shook her hand. "Thank you for all you've done."

"Yes," said Don. "This has been very helpful."

Christiana's arms were wrapped around my waist. "Are we going home now? Can I have a treat for being good?"

"Yes. You've been very patient, Christiana," I said.

Cookie in hand, Christiana crawled into the van, and we headed home. I thought she would be exhausted. We had gotten up earlier than usual to make the hour drive to the hospital that morning. But Christiana was in a silly mood, singing and talking.

Don hadn't said much since we left the office. I could tell he was disturbed. "Is something the matter?" I asked. My extroverted need to "talk things out" made me think he might need to talk.

He shook his head and glanced back at Christiana. "Later," he said. Tears filled his eyes, and he squeezed my hand.

I quickly looked out at the road.

Christiana began to talk to several pretend test-takers, herself in the role of the test administrator. Playacting was a common way she processed whatever had happened during her day.

"Okay, now we will have lunch," Christiana said to her patients. "You may have anything you want. Pizza and ice cream? Okay. Who wants to pray? Ashley? Okay.

"Dear God, thank you for us to take tests today and thank you for the love and thank you for Jesus Christ to come and be born in a stable. Amen. That was very good. . . ."

I stopped listening. Christiana's prayer repeated in my thoughts. *Thank you for the tests . . . for the love . . . for Jesus. Thank you, thank you, thank you.* I smiled. What was the value of jobs or even independent living or marriage in light of the realities of God's love and Jesus Christ "born in a stable."

As I let the simple faith expressed by Christiana's prayer fill me, I felt God prying her loose from my fear-filled grasp. She was not my child to control. She was God's child. She did not need to fulfill my dreams for her. God had a plan and a purpose for her life, a first-rate plan that we would discover together.

Reflections

We all have assumed expectations for our children's lives. Are we willing to allow God to guide them in different directions than what we might plan? The desire within our children to please us as parents is often so strong that we can unknowingly thwart God's plans for them if we do not consciously acknowledge and let go of our expectations for their lives.

Prayer

Dear God, help me to release my children from my crippling dreams for them. Help me to encourage them to seek your plan for their lives even if it means something different than what I imagine. Strengthen my faith in your love for them, which is so much greater than my own, for I must believe in your love if I am to have peace about giving them into your care and guidance. Thank you for the privilege and joy of holding your children in loving stewardship during these brief growing-up years. Amen.

Day 28

NOT AFRAID TO SHINE

O LORD, our Lord,
> how majestic is your name in all the earth! . . .
When I consider your heavens,
> the work of your fingers,
the moon and the stars,
> which you have set in place,
what is man that you are mindful of him,
> the son of man that you care for him?
You made him a little lower than the heavenly beings
> and crowned him with glory and honor.
> > —Psalm 8:1, 3–5

But Jesus called the children to him and said, "Let the little children come to me, and do not hinder them, for the kingdom of God belongs to such as these."

> —Luke 18:16

Why had I agreed, even asked, to share several of my devotional essays with our Sunday school class? I tossed a sipper cup into the dish drainer and plunged a pitcher into soapy water, splashing suds onto my sweatshirt. I huffed.

"Is something wrong?" Don asked.

"Oh, I wish I hadn't said I would teach class tomorrow."

"Why not?"

"The devotionals are meaningful to me, but why do I think others will be able to relate to the lessons? And what about the single people in the class or the couples without children? I don't want them to feel left out. I don't know."

"You'll do fine. You've had quite a bit of positive feedback on the essays already. They'll love them."

I smiled. It was hard to resist the charms of my greatest fan. "Thanks."

I swished my hand in the water, fishing for an elusive jar lid. Don hugged me and kissed my cheek before heading downstairs to the office.

"Mommy," Hannah skipped into the kitchen, "can we have a show?"

"Hmm? I'm sorry, Hannah, I wasn't listening."

"Can Christiana and I have a show?"

"I guess so. What kind of show did you have in mind?"

"Mostly a dancing show. We've been practicing."

The melody of the "Dance of the Sugar Plum Fairy" floated down the hall from Hannah's room. Hannah was dressed in red tights, her frilly slip, and her ballet-shoe house slippers. For the past three weeks, ever since a friend had given the girls the tape of *The Nutcracker* for Christmas, we had been treated to a show every couple of days.

"All right. But not too long. You girls need baths yet tonight."

"Okay." Hannah's voice dragged with disappointment.

"I do enjoy your shows Hannah; it's just that Mommy's tired tonight." I smiled, and Hannah regained some of her bounce.

"Let me finish the dishes. I'll be there in a minute." I retrieved the wayward lid and drained the water.

Hannah met me at the intersection of the kitchen, hall, and living room with the tape player in hand. "You and Papa sit on the couch."

Don came through the kitchen door, his eyes alight with excitement. He bent down to Hannah's level and said, "I hear there's a fancy show going on at the Boggs' house tonight."

Hannah tilted her head in pleased recognition and put her hands on her hips. In her best stage-manager voice, she said, "Papa, it's time to start. Hurry up and sit down."

Don sat next to me on the couch. Sitting down felt good.

The music began. The opening fanfare of the "March of the Toy Soldiers" began. Hannah and Christiana bounded into the room. Christiana displayed her matching red tights and slip ensemble. They pointed their toes and circled their arms over their heads as they leaped and ran back and forth across the room in joyful abandon. Their raised eyebrows, tight smiles, and the exaggerated sweeps of their arms reflected the dozens of times they had viewed Tchaikovsky's Christmas classic.

On one pass, they bumped shoulders and fell down into a heap of giggles and white lace. Through the "Waltz of the Flowers" and the "Dance of the Sugar Plum Fairy," they spun and tiptoed with chins held high. Another bump sent them into reams of laughter. The rest of the show was punctuated with giggles and guffaws every time they looked at each other. At the final bows, their breathless smiles stretched the curves of their cheeks to bursting.

I clapped hard, trying to simulate an audience of thousands. "That was terrific!"

"Bravo! Bravo!" Don stood and applauded double time.

The pleased glow in their eyes warmed my heart. I wondered when the last time was that I had experienced such pure pleasure in another's approval. Perhaps not since I was a child.

Reflections

Do you *know* that God delights in you? We often focus on our faults and imperfections, imagining that we are somewhat of a disappointment to God. But God made us just as we are, unique in personality, appearance, and giftedness, a delight in the Father's eyes.

Prayer

Dear God, I am your child, but at times it's hard to imagine that you feel for me the kind of delighted affection I feel for my children. But you do! When I listen to your "Bravo!" I am free to be me with a personality you delight in. I am free to share the gifts you have given me. Help me to dance to your music today and experience the abundant joy you want for me. In Jesus' name, amen.

Day 29

It's Not Yours

*"[The kingdom of heaven is] like a man going on a journey,
who called his servants and entrusted his property to them."*
—Matthew 25:14

*But godliness with contentment is great gain. For we brought
nothing into the world, and we can take nothing out of it. But
if we have food and clothing, we will be content with that.*
—1 Timothy 6:6–8

The crackling protest of our sticky front door being jarred open drew my attention from my computer screen. I glanced at my watch, not believing that it was time for my daughters to be home from school.

"Mo-om." The call was Hannah's unmistakable I'm-starved-for-a-snack-after-school voice.

I finished the sentence I was typing, clicked "save," and called, "I'm in here, Honey."

A second slam of the door meant that Christiana had also arrived home from a hard day of schoolwork and playground negotiation.

Both girls followed my voice into the living room. Hannah unloaded her backpack onto the floor, sauntered to my side, and leaned on my shoulder. I gave her a side squeeze and scratched her back.

Christiana trotted across the living room and began depositing a week's collection of school treasures onto the table.

"How was your day?" I asked. "Are things going better with Becky and Jerrika?" The week had been a battle of conflicting values for Christiana. The bickering and mean exclusivity of a couple of the other girls in her class had upset her to the point of lost sleep earlier in the week.

Christiana placed before me a show-and-tell doll and said, "It's better."

No further explanation was forthcoming, only an after-school offering of two handfuls of smiley-face-graded papers and a blue and pink elephant-shaped change purse. Then she pulled out a Ziploc® bag containing an exploded glue bottle and a couple dozen crayons. This unusual phenomenon distracted me from the friend crisis.

Having emptied her pack, Christiana walked on into the kitchen as if there was nothing unusual about the white sea of floating crayons. "What's for snack?" she asked.

Hannah rolled away from my side and followed her sister.

"I think there's some pretzels in the cabinet and apples in the fruit drawer."

I picked up the corner of the plastic bag; it would take too much effort to salvage the crayons. "What happened to your glue, Christiana?"

"I took the lid off and forgot when I put it away," she said and marched back into the living room with a protruding lower lip. "Is that all there is for snack?"

"I gave you money for a cookie at lunch, Christiana. And if you get your room clean before supper, you may have dessert. That's plenty of sweets for one day."

Christiana stomped through the kitchen and disappeared into the backyard. The mention of lunch money reminded me that I had given Christiana two dollar bills to pay for a $1.40 lunch and a 15¢ cookie. I unzipped the elephant purse and felt inside for my 45¢ change, but none offered itself. I wondered if my sweet-toothed child had finished her lunch with four cookies, or perhaps a fifty cent bag of candy? I shook her book bag to make sure the change wasn't there.

I walked through the kitchen where Hannah was munching on an apple and into the backyard. Christiana was in full swing.

"Christiana, where's the change from your lunch money?"

"I don't know."

"Christiana, I gave you two dollars for lunch and a cookie. You should have brought me back forty-five cents. We talked about it this morning. Remember?"

"I don't know, okay!"

The rhythmic thump of a swing-set leg pounded the ground with frightening force.

"Christiana, stop swinging for a minute. We need to talk."

Christiana's face twisted into a defensive wall as she slapped her tennis shoes against the packed dirt. Four passes later, she sat earthbound, her arms wrapped around the swing chains as if they were a life raft and I was preparing to wrench her away and throw her into a raging sea.

"Christiana, you need to tell me what happened to the extra money. Did you lose it?"

"No!"

"Did you buy something more or different than the cookie we agreed on this morning?"

"No."

"Is the money at school then?"

"No."

"Then what did you do with the money?"

Christiana twisted the swing back and forth, staring at her pivotal toe. "I gave it to Becky and Jerrika."

"Why, Honey?"

"So they would be my friends."

I squatted down and took hold of the sides of the swing, waiting until Christiana looked up.

"Christiana, do you think that is a good way to make friends?"

"No." Her tone implied compliance but not conviction.

"Christiana, if you have to give someone money to be your friend, then that person isn't really your friend. A friend likes you for who you are, not for what you give her." I knew my words, although true, were a feather on the scale weighing against her passion to be accepted by the girls in her class.

"And the money was not yours, Christiana. The money was Mama's and Papa's. You mustn't give away something that is not yours. That's sort of like stealing."

Christiana's face lit with indignation. "I did not steal. You gave me the money."

"Christiana, I gave you the money for a specific purpose and all that was left over was to come back to me."

Christiana's mouth stood open as if she would speak, but then she dropped her head and stared once again at her toes. Christiana had many behavior struggles, but overall she was an honest child with a highly functional conscience.

"I'm sorry, Mommy. Do you forgive me?"

"Of course I forgive you, Christiana. And will you bring the change back next time?"

Christiana smiled. "Of course, Mommy."

Reflections

God has given us abilities, relationships, possessions, and time. As servants of God, we are stewards, not owners, of these gifts. He has given us these blessings not only for the purpose of our enjoyment but also to glorify God and serve others.

Prayer

Dear God, help me not to give away my time and talents because of the pressures people put on me or to solely satisfy my own desires. May I always look to you for instruction on how you want the stuff of my life to be used. May I be generous to others as you have been generous with me. Amen.

Day 30

HE PIZZA OF LIFE

Jesus said to them, . . . "It is my Father who gives you the true bread from heaven. For the bread of God is he who comes down from heaven and gives life to the world. . . . I am the bread of life. He who comes to me will never go hungry. . . . I am the living bread. . . . If [anyone] eats of this bread, he will live forever."

—John 6:32–35, 51

I let out a relaxing sigh. Sitting still in the passenger seat and listening to the monotonous hum of the van's tires against the pavement felt like a treat. That's how busy my day had been; zipping along the interstate, doing nothing and listening to nothing felt terrific.

Miraculously, for the past hour, all three children had been looking at books. In fact, they had been so quiet that I checked a couple of times to make sure they were still there. I hated to interrupt the enchanted moment, but it was time to stop for supper, and we needed to decide where we were going to eat. I pulled the *Exit Authority* from under my seat and flipped through the pages to find the restaurant listings for the upcoming exits.

"Where should we stop for supper, Honey?"

Before Don could answer, Nathaniel, the ever-ready-to-eat teenaged "honey" chimed in, "I thought we were going to have pizza."

"You want pizza *again?*"

"Of course." Nathaniel looked at me as if he couldn't believe my disbelief.

"How about you, Hannah? Do you want pizza again?"

Hannah looked up from her book. "Sure."

"But you've had pizza for the past three nights," I said.

"We did?" Hannah rolled her eyes up and to the left, accessing her culinary memories of the past few days.

"Remember, Tuesday evening instead of eating meatloaf, you finished off the pizza leftovers from the weekend. Then, on Wednesday, Papa took you all out for pizza because I was held up with jury duty. Thursday, Papa and I went out, and the sitter fixed you pizza."

Hannah nodded. "Oh yeah, I remember. That's okay. I'll eat pizza again."

I shook my head. "Christiana, how about you? Do you want pizza?"

"Yum, yum! Let's have pizza!" she answered.

Nathaniel put a marker in his book and leaned forward to plead his pizza case. "I thought you said that if we helped get ready for the garage sale you would buy pizza for everyone with some of the money."

"Yes, I did say that, but I wasn't sure then that we were going to be visiting Grandma and Grandpa this weekend, and I just didn't think you would want pizza four days in a row."

"Of course we want pizza," Nathaniel said. "I don't ever get tired of pizza—well, maybe frozen pizza—but not the good kind. And pizza is like a complete meal with all of the food groups. You know, crust for the bread, tomato sauce for vegetables, cheese for milk, and, of course, pepperoni for meat. Besides, it tastes really good."

I reached over and rubbed Don's shoulder. "Driver's privilege, Honey. What do you say?"

"It's okay with me."

"All right. Pizza it is."

I flipped through the *Exit Authority,* encouraged by the applause of the backseat peanut gallery.

"Mommy, you're the best mommy in the world," Christiana said.

Reflections

Jesus as nourishment for our souls is not just one of many choices we can take or leave. To maintain the very life of our souls, we need to partake every day of God's Spirit and feast on Christ's love, peace, strength, and wisdom with the hungry passion of a child.

Prayer

Dear God, fill my heart with an insatiable craving for you. Help me to never tire of the flavor of your presence. Be the delicious sustenance that fills my being, for you are the living bread who nourishes my soul to eternal life. Amen.

HE LIGHT OF THE WORLD

Your word is a lamp to my feet
and a light for my path.
—Psalm 119:105

In the beginning was the Word . . . In him was life, and that
life was the light of men.

—John 1:1, 4

I [Jesus] am the light of the world.

—John 9:5

My crocuses were blooming. Their delicate purple faces were shining heralds of the promise of spring, of sunlight until bedtime, of the radiant warmth penetrating and restoring my winter-weary body. For months, I had closed the blinds before supper against the darkness, but tonight the blinds were open, and we were eating dinner by the rosy hues of setting sunlight.

Christiana's excited voice pulled me away from my spring musings back to last evening's leftovers. "Mom, can we go outside with flashlights after supper?"

"Please?" Hannah added.

In the fall, kids shiver and pull out their sweatshirts when the temperature drops to sixty-eight. But in the spring, they put on short sleeves and kick off their shoes in response to the same sixty-eight degrees. I knew how they felt. I didn't want this delightful day of outdoor bliss to end either.

"I suppose that would be all right."

Don nodded his okay.

I glanced at my watch. The youth meeting at church started in ten minutes. "Nathaniel, we need to get going. I'll be back in a bit."

The pinks, yellows, and oranges of sunset-colored clouds floated down into the horizon as I drove to the church. It was fundraiser sign-up night, so I walked Nathaniel into the meeting and copied the dates of four work opportunities.

On my drive home, the lovely hues of the sunset gave way to the garish glare of streetlights and headlights. When I climbed out of the car, pinpoints of starlight pricked the blackened sky.

The house was quiet and empty. I hit the talk button on the intercom connecting the basement office to the upstairs.

"Don, I'm home."

"Hi, Honey."

I was going to ask where Christiana and Hannah were, when I heard laughter coming from the backyard. Out the picture window, I could see the images of two children, whose shadows jumped in and out of dancing pools of darting white light. I couldn't hear the conversation, but their giggles and shouts told me they were having a grand time. I watched for several minutes. Like a pair of oversized lightening bugs, I could trace their paths by the stop and start, swing around, up and down motion of their flashlight beams.

I checked the time. Tomorrow was a school day, and I knew the soles of their bare feet needed washing before crawling into bed. I knocked on the window. The swaying lights stopped. I motioned for the silhouettes to come in. A moment later, two dim white beams illuminated the path toward home.

My red-faced, bright-eyed pair of energized children tumbled into the quiet house, heralded by an operetta of giggled and panted song. I'd never heard a more delightful duet of "Jesus Loves Me" clap and stomp style.

"Very good! Now, off with the flashlights. You need to get into the bath before bedtime."

Hannah's shoulders dropped as she switched off her light. "Already?"

"Yes. It's a school night, you know."

Christiana's bouncing feet hadn't stopped. "I'll go first." She handed me her flashlight and skipped down the hall.

"It seems like you girls had a great time outside."

Hannah tilted her head and nodded slowly like an aged sage. "Yes. I think it's good to look at things differently sometimes."

She handed me her light.

I looked at her flashlight in my hand. Perhaps, when I got Hannah and Christiana to bed, I would take a walk.

Reflections

The light of the Holy Spirit can fill us from head to toe, calming, warming, healing, restoring, and cleansing us. The light of the Spirit goes ahead of us into each day, filling all of the spaces where we will be, lighting our path, illuminating opportunities to love, and clarifying places of potential stumbling. The light of Christ can spotlight eternal moments of God's revelation and surround even the dark places with the reality of God's immanent, loving presence.

Prayer

Dear God, you are my light. Sometimes your light is beautiful like the gentle colors of the sunset. Sometimes your light is warm and penetrating like the rays of the sun. Sometimes your light illuminates my path and keeps me from stumbling. Help me not only to bask in the glory of your light but also to seek out ways of taking your light into the darkness. For when

I shine your light into the dark places, things look different than I expect, and then I experience the joy of discovery for myself and others. Help me to realize that as long as you are my light, I have nothing to fear from the darkness. Amen.

CONCLUSION

Parenting is one of the most challenging and rewarding experiences that we'll have during this life. God has given us this extraordinary opportunity to learn about ourselves and grow in our faith while holding gently, in open hands, God's very own children to raise in the way of the Lord. I challenge you to see your relationship with the children in your life as a sweet training ground for relating to God.

Sometimes we can implement this integrative parenting perspective by simply asking God to keep our minds and hearts alert to the lessons he wants to teach us even within our hurried moments. In the harried seasons of life, we can take a few minutes before we fall asleep at night to ask God what lesson he has sought to teach us while we have endeavored to teach our young ones.

At other stages of life, we may have time to keep a journal to write down the insights God gives us in relating to our children. This record can be a precious keepsake for years to come.

Finding a friend with whom to exchange parenting stories and spiritual insights is another wonderful way to hide in our hearts the revelations God gives us through our children.

In all moments, let us seek first God's kingdom in ourselves and our families. For Jesus has promised that if we seek, we will find, if we ask, it will be given, and if we knock, the door will be opened to us.

At times, a mother's life can be anything but inspiring—2 A.M. feedings, loneliness, no vacation days. Even the best intentions of raising God-fearing, obedient, happy kids can spiral downward in the midst of her chaos.

Calm in My Chaos takes an honest, biblical look at a mother's world and offers practical advice on common experiences including:

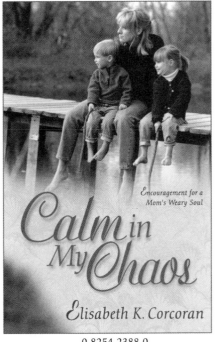

- Being content in every circumstance
- Modeling God-like characteristics
- Making and keeping friends
- Being the "real" you

0-8254-2388-0

"Readers, especially mothers, will . . . relate to Elisabeth's words. In fact, she shares so many personal experiences that readers may find themselves thinking of her as a close friend. *Calm in My Chaos* . . . is very well written and beautifully expressed."

—Joi M. Lasnick, *My ParenTime*

"A wonderful encouragement. . . . *[Calm in My Chaos]* takes the Word and weaves it through the experiences of a mother's day. A wonderful book."

—Carol Jo Brazo
author of *No Ordinary Home*

"Mom, read and be blessed!"

—Lorraine Pintus
author of *Diapers, Pacifiers, and Other Holy Things*